Mewlogy

Grieving a Very Special Cat

Written and Illustrated
by K.S. Schurr

VikinMunk

Publishing

Lincoln, Nebraska

MEWLOGY: GRIEVING A VERY SPECIAL CAT

©2020 Karen S. Schurr. All Rights Reserved.

Published by VinkinMunk Publishing. Photos and stories are from the personal collections of the author, or cited according to requirements.

For contact information, visit www.VinkinMunkPublishing.com

Hardcover, full color: 978-1-7342067-1-5
Paperback, full color: 978-1-7342067-2-2
Paperback, black and white: 978-1-7342067-3-9
Mobi: 978-1-7342067-4-6
EPUB: 978-1-7342067-5-3

Cataloging-in-Publication Data on file with the publisher.
Library of Congress Control Number on file with the publisher.

Publishing and Production by Concierge Marketing Inc.

Printed and bound in the United States of America
10 9 8 7 6 5 4 3 2 1

To Jim,
the light of my life,
who has trained lots of cats

To Lois "Lolo" Gowler,
who is responsible for starting all this

To Barbara "The Buckster" Stock,
who is my family, audience, and editor

mew·lo·gy (MYOO - luh - jee) n.

**1. A piece of writing that praises a cat highly,
typically one who has just died.**

Did you ever think you would be reading a cat's biography? My guess is no, but yet, here you are.

"Cat" was likely among the first twenty words you spoke. Once you understood the connection between the name and the animal, that iconic outline was forever branded into your brain.

On the Rosetta Stone, carved in 196 BC, the ancient Egyptian word for cat is written as follows:

The first three hieroglyphs display the sound "miw"—derived from the signature "miaow"—followed by a picture of a cat.

So, obviously, felines have been a part of our lives and global culture for a long, long time. They have been in my own life since I was three years old. Meet me and my kitty, George:

Cats have come and gone from my world for decades, and I was thrilled to coexist with them, but I didn't become truly aware of how they helped me enrich my days and cope with my sorrow until Kozmo arrived. He was something special. His time on the planet was brief, one of many things humans and animals have in common.

The following tale began as the biography of an exceptional feline companion, but instead gave rise to more of an autobiography. This book is a chronology of the past twenty-five years of my own life, peppered with the wisdom, strength of character, and comfort I've gained from sharing my days with domesticated cats.

Pets intimately share our lives and can become surrogates for our closest family members. The relatively short life spans of our animal companions test our mettle, but can provide us with the experience of profound loss, teaching us valuable life lessons along the way. Practice sessions of grief help us recognize the priceless value of our loved ones. Familiarity with loss steels us, lets us reflect more upon our past experiences, and helps us recognize a familiar path to revitalization, one based on what we know is inevitable but survivable.

The grief that came with Kozmo's loss was familiar to me. I had already dealt with the deaths of my only sibling and my father, but, by the time Kozmo left me, I had developed an appreciative understanding of the cycle of life, which I continue to build on as I mature and lose loved ones. That experience led me to write this story in hopes that it will soften the blow of our ultimate mortal destiny for you, as it did for me.

Chapter 1:
Feb. 1998, Kozmo Arrives

Prior to Kozmo, Jim and I had rescued a nine-month-old Russian Blue cat named Gilly, the first pet of our marriage. Gilly was the name of my cousin's Siamese when I was eleven. After hearing that unusual name for a cat, I decided I would keep it in mind for the first one I parented twenty-five years later. Jim, who had raised lots of cats, felt it would be in Gilly's best interest to share his days with a roommate, so we paired him with a tuxedo-shirted tabby we called Dot, in honor of my mother, Dorothy.

When Gilly was eight, he was diagnosed with a brain tumor. The specialist who diagnosed the tumor recommended not reviving Gilly from his exploratory surgery anesthetic, and we followed this advice. That left Dot without a feline companion. It was obvious from the way she listlessly roamed the house that she missed her partner, as did we, so vetting a replacement was required.

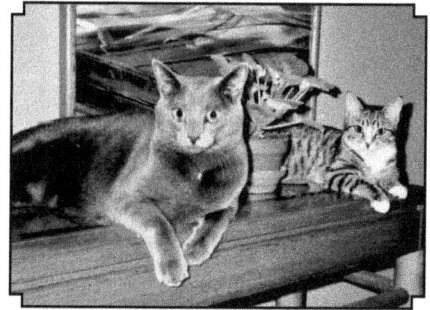

Gilly and the Dot

We had never considered a purebred cat for fear of genetic problems and excessive costs, but once we got to know our friends' cat, Buck Hibbs, we were sold on getting one of the same Abyssinian breed, a variety often termed the "clowns of the cat world" due to their personality.

We admired Buck's slight, muscular build and enjoyed his outlandish behavior whenever we visited his owner's home. Buck lived every day to the fullest and loved to be the center of attention, doing whatever it took to achieve and maintain that status. We were intrigued that a pet would actually challenge our ability to keep pace, and thus the search began.

Ruddy Abyssinian Buck Hibbs

We figured the best place to look for our own Abby was at the local annual cat show, a hotbed of choices in a single location and a magnet for eccentrics and their sophisticated yet somewhat bizarre cat pageantry. As we passed the pens of newborns, one kitten immediately caught our attention, since his tiny face was pressed against the grill of his cage. As we paused to get a better look, his owner picked him up, thrust him at me, and introduced him as "Hot Shot."

Our first look at Kozmo
(Photo by Peter Hasselbom)

hot·shot (hŏt-shŏt') *n.*

1. *Slang* **One of impressive skill and daring, highly successful and self-assured.**

2. A nonstop freight train.

Both would prove to be accurate descriptions.

As he was handed off to me, "Hot Shot" instantly started purring, or should I say, "rattling." The sound was like the valve clatter of a car engine. He clamped his claws onto the front of my coat and started kneading me with the expertise of a baker. Jim and I were completely enamored with his charm and the pleading look he shared with us, begging us to take him in. It was a done deal, simple as that.

After a quick trip home, Dot laid her eyes on the new addition to the family. Quite a difference from the hulking, eighteen-pound alpha-moggy she had been bunking with for years. I could imagine a caption bubble over her head conveying a groan of "Oy vey."

Now came the hardest part of pet ownership, that of naming the beast. Keep in mind, the year 1998 was the last season of the sitcom **Seinfeld**, one of our favorite humorous escapes from reality

Dot meets Kozmo

at the time. We decided to christen our new arrival "Kozmo" after Cosmo Kramer, known for his sliding bursts through Jerry's apartment door and, most notably, his lack of any visible support. It seemed fitting.

The spelling was kept as unique as we felt Kozmo to be, even on the first day of his adoption. That very day, Dot licked the dust off her new little companion. She was perfectly willing to accept him, cat show smells be damned. She began his training by showing him the all-important location of the litter box. We were all naïve in thinking he would instantly understand it was where he should thereafter do his "business" and were stunned as we helplessly watched him squat before us and take his first poop on our new family room carpet.

Although secure enough to share that intimate event with us, it was obvious he was a bit off-balance. We found him the next morning, huddled in a ball behind the piano after his first solo night in a strange place, separated from his littermates. It was likely this stress and his immature immune system that caused him to contract an upper respiratory infection. What started as a runny nose and sneezing quickly led to ulcers in his eyeballs, little depressions like dimples on a golf ball.

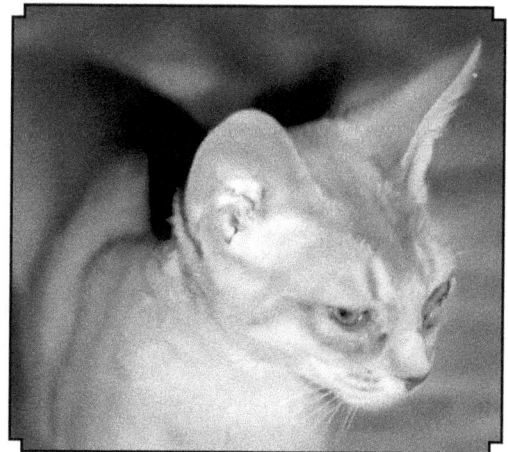

Kozmo gets a cold

Thus, it was off to the veterinarian. It was there our impression of Kozmo's significance was substantiated by unbiased cat experts. When the clinic's receptionist took a look at Koz's behavior in his pet carrier, she exclaimed, "Now that kitty's got an attitude!" (though she may have meant "catitude"). The vet herself was equally smitten with his spirited personality. She prescribed treatment for the little guy and told us he should be back to normal in a short time, though it took weeks to heal his indented eyes.

Our next few months were spent observing the development of Kozmo's character, and Dot's upper limit for mayhem was exhaustively stretched.

Kozmo's first notable stunt was an odd form of bronco busting. No horses in the house? No problem. He picked the obvious surrogate: Dot. Unfortunately, this feat was a singular event, witnessed only by me. Consequently, the need arose for a thoughtfully rendered illustration of this far-fetched situation.

I distinctly remember the term "YEEHAW!" flashing through my brain as I watched this fleeting spectacle take place.

This instance was yet another indication that Kozmo was either an exceptional kitten or an alien life form. We began to watch his behaviors closer, since we were so entertained by him and never knew when he would do something extraordinary. This attention played right into his need to be the focal point of both human and feline eyes. Yes, Dot was just as captivated by him as we were.

Chapter 2: May 1998, Adolescence

The period of human adolescence, between the ages of about ten and nineteen years, allows growth and development from infancy to maturity. Assuming human and cat years are relative, this period in Kozmo's life would equate to between 0.7 and 1.4 years of age (in human terms).

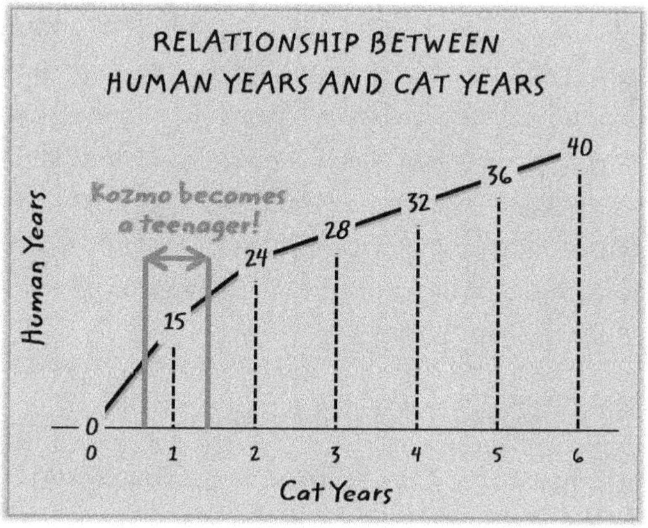

RELATIONSHIP BETWEEN
HUMAN YEARS AND CAT YEARS
Human Years
Kozmo becomes a teenager!
0
15
24
28
32
36
40
0
1
2
3
4
5
6
Cat Years

Compounding his internal maturity chaos, Kozmo was a red-blooded, all-American tomcat one day and two beans lighter the next. Yes, following the recommendations of our local animal shelter, we had our vet "farm his potatoes," performing a gonadectomy to ensure his "de-broification." In other words, we had him neutered. As if that wasn't enough torment and humiliation for him, this was also a convenient time to get his front paws declawed, which was a huge decision.

We had decided Kozmo's destiny to be that of a captive housecat in order to extend his chances of a long, heathy life. In the short time since his adoption, his energy had accelerated exponentially, as had the amount of ripped window shades, shredded woodwork, and marred furniture around the house, due to him scaling his surroundings like a spider monkey on crack cocaine. After much deliberation of the pros and cons of having his front claws removed, we decided it was in all of our best interests. After all, he would still have his rear claws for protecting himself in challenging situations, should he accidentally get outdoors.

When we opened the door of his pet carrier at home after his surgery, he charged out in his familiar fashion of going nowhere fast. He puffed up stem to stern, turned sideways to make himself look larger, and flashed us a scary face with riveted eye contact, confirming our suspicions: he was expecting further attacks on his person.

He appeared to be unaffected by his vet visit, but we were well aware of how animals mask their weakness, hiding it from potential predators. We knew he was probably hurting more than he let on. It was definitely time for intense cuddling and fawning praise, encouraging him to forget the last twenty-four hours and focus on the moment. Luckily for us, the miniscule attention span of our seven-month-old kitten worked in our favor. He was putty in our hands in no time, as evidenced by his signature clattering purr.

Early Peculiar Tendencies

The days of Kozmo's adolescence were filled with new learning experiences and the development of some odd preferences and habits. His first notable fixation was on all things yeasty. One morning, while preparing a breakfast bagel on the kitchen counter, I momentarily left my food unattended. Upon my return, Kozmo was sitting by the toaster, eyeballing my prize. He took one quick look at me over his shoulder, made a healthy

chomp in the side of the bagel, and thrust it with a horizontal spin toward the center of the kitchen, as if it was a Frisbee. As soon as it left his teeth, he sprang off the counter, following the bagel to the floor.

He bit into it once again and feverishly tried to escape my scrambling attempt to reclaim my pilfered brekkie. Thankfully, the weight of the bagel, the size of his small mouth, and his general lack of Frisbee coordination all played into my favor. I caught him in time and won this particular contest of will and wits.

Not long after the attempted bagel heist, there was another incident that further clarified Kozmo's "kneady" obsession. This occurred when Jim and I both caught him sliding an entire loaf of bread along the living room floor. Since we initially got to observe this without his knowledge, we were able to see how he managed to achieve such a challenging objective.

He positioned himself over the top of the loaf lengthwise, barely clearing it. Then he grabbed the cellophane wrapper's end under his chin, tugging the load forward as he slowly walked over the top of it. Inch by inch he pulled it, heading in the direction of the upstairs bedrooms. Before long, he noticed us watching him and fled the crime scene without his booty, no doubt fully aware of his wrongdoing.

The Need for Disciplinary Action

It quickly became obvious to us that it was necessary to nip Kozmo's growing rap sheet of counterproductive behaviors in the bud, so we drew upon our previous experiences as cat owners to train him in traditional ways. Our first punitive effort was to catch Kozmo in the act and spray him with water. The perfect opportunity came shortly after the bread bandit bungle. I caught him sitting in the kitchen sink, licking drops of water from the tap. I turned the steady droplets into a full-strength stream over his head and supplemented the punishment with screams of "No, no, no!"

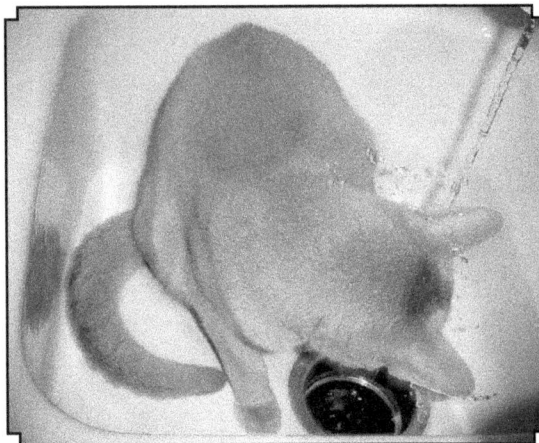

Kozmo in the kitchen sink

Not only was Kozmo unfazed by the shouting and sudden rush of cold water in his ear, the water beaded off him as if he were a duck. So our cat was born with a protective coating? This obsession with water was unquenchable and proved to be a part of his shtick thenceforth.

After being introduced to plumbing fixtures, Koz proceeded to search his domain for all potential water outlets. This included the upstairs bathroom sinks, where he adapted his style of consumption to dipping his paw in a stream of water and licking it off after it was sopping wet.

What became known as "the old dip and sip" modus operandi also applied to the shower stall. Whenever we took a shower, Koz would hop up on the toilet and carefully align his flight path with the top of the shower door.

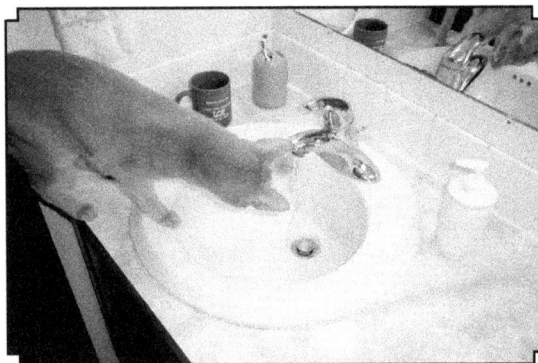

Kozmo in the bathroom sink

Shower Jump Position 1   Shower Jump Position 2   Shower Jump Position 3

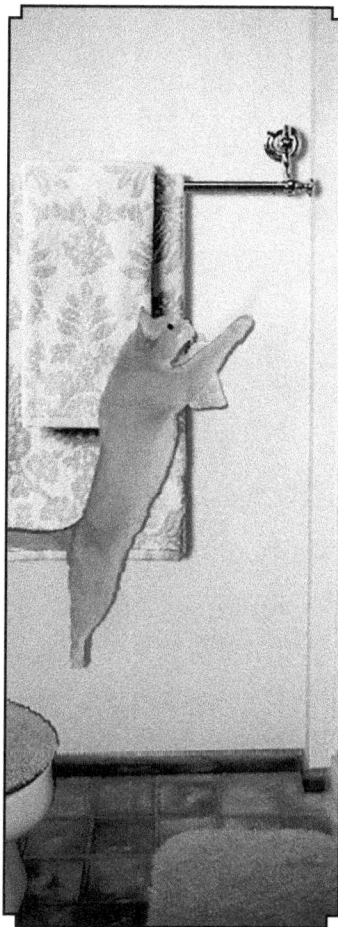

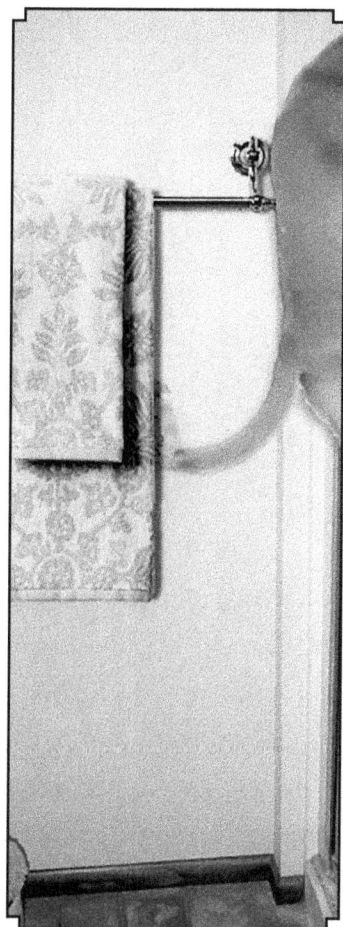

Then he would jump for all he was worth toward the door. Note his impeccable form in the air.

After his initial contact would come an impressive feline pull-up to get at least three of his paws on top of the inch-wide door. He would dip and sip from the showerhead right in front of us until he was sated, then jump to the floor and go on his merry way. One hasn't lived until one has showered with one's cat.

Kozmo and Jim get refreshed

The "Blessing" of the Dinner Plate

Early in cat ownership, humans must discover their own level of tolerance for sharing living quarters with animals. Like it or not, surfaces within the house and the air we breathe therein are peppered with feline molecules. For health reasons, if for nothing else, standards must be set defining when a pet has crossed the line of hygiene acceptability. For us, there came a day when this boundary was distinctly evident.

It would be great if all pussy cats were enveloped in a shrink wrap outer coating that would keep all loose hair, dander, saliva, and other miscellaneous microbes from interacting with our own surroundings. There may be another planet where that is possible, but it's certainly not ours. Since Kozmo didn't wear pants, we understood that when he was sitting anywhere in our house, his most personal and polished orifice was making direct contact with whatever surface he was planted on (floors, furniture, etc.). For some reason, this seems acceptable to me, even though I wince as I think about it now.

I was preparing dinner one night and had set the table for our evening meal. As I turned to transfer a serving bowl from the kitchen to the table, I was greeted with the ravenous eyes of Kozmo, his butt planted squarely in the center of the plate, which was mere seconds away from holding my steaming meal. As prized as an actual photograph of this disgusting event would have been, the time it took me to manually draw it on paper helped me to ease the angst I still feel vividly, even to this day.

I can't express how quickly my mind flashed through all the instances when this same incident could have occurred without my knowledge. Over the past few months, Koz had been caught in the act of many unsavory deeds, but this had to be one of the most revolting. I hovered my face over his and shrieked as loud as I could: "No, no, no! Off the table or you are a goner!" His reaction to this menacing threat was one of total boredom. He lethargically turned away from me and casually padded off the table to the floor.

Revised Punitive Measures

We had known for some time that Kozmo was fearless, but had deluded ourselves into extreme denial so as not to face the fact that we could not, by any means whatsoever, control his bad or good behavior. He was so plucky he would willingly submit to the tiny clutching hands of babies, relishing the pain of the wee fiends' unyielding grips tangled in his coat.

Once, when Koz was seated peacefully on the living room floor, I watched a two-year-old boy grab his loose, furry chest coat with both hands and pull in opposite directions without Kozmo even breaking a single vibration of his purr. He was amazingly unflappable, especially around children.

Realizing we were without a single disciplinary measure with which to contain our little rapscallion, we were at our wit's end. Luckily, in commiserating with cat-owning friends battling similar frustrations, we were told of a homemade, tried-and-true deterrent.

Our saving grace came in the form of an empty soda can with coins in it. We called it the "Kitty Behavior-Aider." We put one in every room of the house so it would be readily accessible in case of any type of feline transgression.

Kozmo loving baby Nick

We were so relieved to have a quick and effective way to get Kozmo's adolescent attention at the instant of wrongdoing, making sure he knew what faux pas he had either intentionally or inadvertently committed. We think the annoying sound of rattling coins against the sides of the aluminum can bothered his hearing.

We have to admit this method just minimized bad behaviors and did not totally stop them, but we somewhat admired that irascible resistance he had to authority and would probably have been saddened if we had actually broken that persistent spirit we had grown to love in him.

Chapter 3:
Dec. 1999, Crises in Catlandia

It was on the threshold of adulthood that Kozmo's constitution was challenged by a mysterious occurrence that would prove life-threatening. Thankfully, our household of two adult humans, one pint-sized tabby, and one possible extraterrestrial had finally reached the point of predictable co-existence after months of semi-successful cat-nurturing efforts. Although Kozmo's manic meddling in human/co-feline activities was troublesome, his curiosity had leveled out to a steady stream of likely behaviors.

Clinking the Kitty Behavior-Aider was usually successful in distracting him from wayward hijinks. Its high-pitched rattle would cause him to run for cover, out of sight until, having forgotten why he was being punished, he would casually rejoin the family unit. We believed it was one such lightning-fast exit that injured him. One evening, just after being banished, he returned to us with a large, bloody wound on his forehead. We didn't actually know what had happened to him, but we thought he may have run with blazing speed under the bed for refuge without lowering his head enough to clear the frame. Oddly, he didn't act as though he was even injured, so we waited until the next day to seek professional advice for how to treat it.

The vet prescribed a topical salve for the wound, and we were relieved the injury merely required a simple treatment, but our hopes for a short recovery for Kozmo were dashed when he started to scratch the wound obsessively with his back claws, quickly expanding its size.

Kozmo gets an ouchie

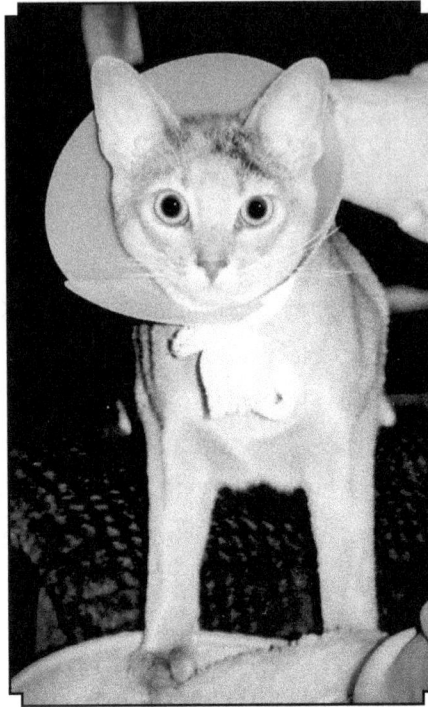

Plan B: "The Cone of Shame"

We took Koz back to the vet, who immediately wrapped his head in the dreaded pet recovery collar. We could tell by the look on Koz's face that this form of animal torture and humiliation was not welcome. When we got him home, he tried to escape his pet carrier in the usual speedy fashion, but got his collar hooked on the side of his cage and ended up tumbling out. After getting to his feet, he slowly raised his head, meeting our eyes with a look of extreme mortification. What on earth had he done to deserve this indignity? We watched as he trudged away from us, head down, shoulders slumped, only to get the collar hooked on the leg of an end table. This was the beginning of a long road ahead.

Plan C: The Cheesecloth Necktie

He had worn the collar only a couple of days before he developed a rash along his neckline from the constant chafing it caused. We designed a stylish cheesecloth necktie for him, thinking it would reduce the friction on his skin, but that was just another irritant to his neck and self-respect. Now, instead of scratching at his head sore with his back claws, he was creating bloody scuffs on the back of his neck.

Plan D: The Custom-Made Tube Socks

What started as a single, quarter-sized forehead ouchie had now become multiple hot spots requiring attention. Our solution to eliminating further skin abrasions was to look straight to the source of the problem: his back claws.

After some awkwardly obtained measurements, sock-drawer searching, creative patterning, and microscopic fashioning, KozSox were created. We slipped the tiny tubes over his back feet and taped them around his ankles for a snug fit. Oddly, he seemed pleased with the design and even posed for a flattering snapshot. Multiple pairs were needed since they had to be changed frequently.

We were so delighted all the wounds were healing and the light at the end of the crisis tunnel was growing larger. However, with every change of KozSox, the tape pulled more and more fur from Kozmo's ankles until those, too, became irritated. We finally had to face the hard fact that a surgical resolution was inevitable.

Koz in taped tube socks

Plan E: Rear Claw-ectomy

We realized Kozmo's good health was ultimately dependent upon having the vet remove his back claws. After walking through the clinic door with him in his pet carrier, we knew he could smell that familiar animal tension in the air. As we handed him, still in his cage, over to the assistant, he rolled his eyes up to meet ours.

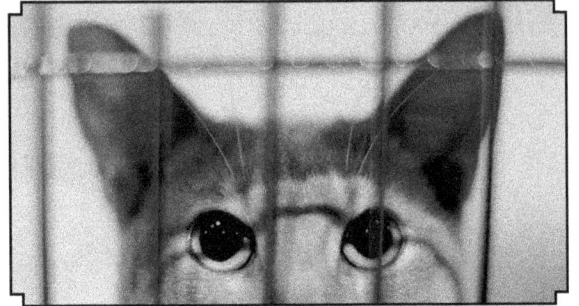

Awaits rear claw-ectomy

He looked as though he knew what was ahead and shamed us with his gaze. It was hard to leave him there after all the efforts we had made over nearly a month to help him, but we had run out of choices.

When we picked him up two days later, he was still a bit groggy, which helped with keeping his back feet away from his multiple sores. He was no longer interested in using his back feet for anything but his familiar trudge through the house. All of his wounds had gone past the itchy phase, and he was finally on the road to recovery.

Another CAT-astrophy

With Kozmo on the mend, we could again split our attention to include his little bunkmate, Dot. She had been his loyal pal as he struggled with Plans A through E, grooming his face, between his ears, the back of his neck, and under his chin as best she could, given she had to do it with the Cone of Shame in her way.

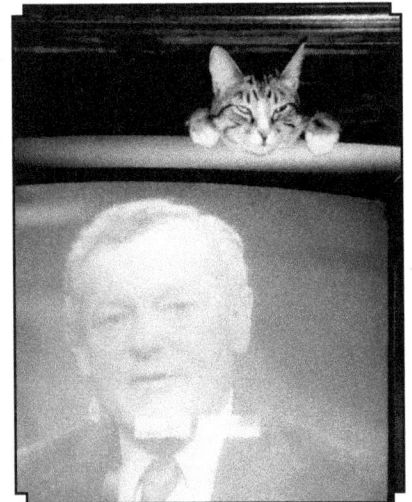

Dot atop newscaster Bob Schieffer

Dot's personality was cloned from that of her namesake, my mother Dorothy. Both had the sweetest of sweet dispositions, were well behaved, and followed the rules. Although Dot was capable of a shenanigan or two, they seldom occurred. She was a perfect foil for Kozmo's overwhelming presence and actually seemed to prefer that station in life.

She was about seven years old at this point, which equates to middle age in the feline world. She had been dealing with a common cat malady of gradual kidney failure for several months, which we had been treating with medication and changes in her diet. With so much of our attention centered on Kozmo, we hadn't noticed Dot's gradual change in weight and strength. Although she was sticking to her normal routine, she seemed slow and weak.

This frailty was abruptly brought to our attention when she tried to jump on a low stool but failed, dropping feebly to the floor. We hadn't realized she was slowly wasting away right under our noses. Both cats ate from the same dish, and, unbeknownst to us, Kozmo had been eating most of it.

The day after her fall, we took her to the vet, who placed her on the examining table/scale. We were shocked to see she weighed barely four pounds. She had always been a small cat, but her weight before her illness had been about seven pounds. She was listless and frail on that day. After the examination, the vet gave us a look we'd never forget just before the bad news: she was in dire straits. She was extremely dehydrated from the near-total loss of kidney function, which had caused her sudden lack of appetite and weight loss. We had both surmised the vet's recommendation for euthanasia before he said it. It was obviously the most humane course of action. This choice had been the one we made when our first cat, Gilly, was diagnosed with brain cancer during exploratory surgery, so it wasn't the first time we were faced with a decision of life or death for a beloved pet.

It also wasn't the first time I'd dealt with death in an intimate way. When I was thirteen, my older brother Denny—then away at college—was killed in a car accident. While my parents were on the late-night journey of two hundred miles to be with him at his deathbed, I was at a fun-filled sleepover with my two best friends, whose parents kept me unaware of the tragedy until I was dropped off at home late the next day. When I walked into our house that morning, I was instantly wrapped in my dad's embrace.

Through his sobs, he said, "Denny is gone." I was in shock through his wake and funeral, as were my parents as we tried to figure out a way to console ourselves. It took me months to fully comprehend that I would never see him again, often dreaming he was still very much a part of my daily life.

When I was twenty years old and attending college in a nearby city, my father died while in the hospital where he was being treated for a diabetes-related heart complication. I received this shocking news by telephone from my weeping mother, another unforeseen and surreal exposure to the instant loss of my very closest family. Dealing with that nebulous lonesomeness left me with a lengthy bout of depression, largely due to being so distant from the comforting presence of my mother while coming to grips with my grief.

These painful thoughts were mixed with those of compassion for Dot, as she lay on the examining table, so fragile, just barely there. We stroked her gently in her favorite spots and spoke softly about what a wonderful friend she was to us in Dotspeak, a special type of pet-talk we reserved for communicating with her and only her. The vet prepared a syringe with an overdose of anesthetic, which he injected into a vein along the inside of her thigh. This caused her to lose consciousness and expire peacefully within seconds of injection. We were warned she might pass with her eyes open, and that was true in her case. Her gaze went vacant. The vet checked for her heartbeat and silently nodded his head. She was "gone."

We returned home with empty hearts and a lighter pet carrier. After setting it down in the entry, Kozmo ran to look at his little buddy through the grill of the cage. She wasn't there. He began a casual search of his realm, no doubt wondering where she was hiding, ready to initiate a tussle or a lickfest, depending on how he read her mood. We snatched him up from his quest and squeezed him between us to absorb his vitality and feel the reassuring vibration of his purr.

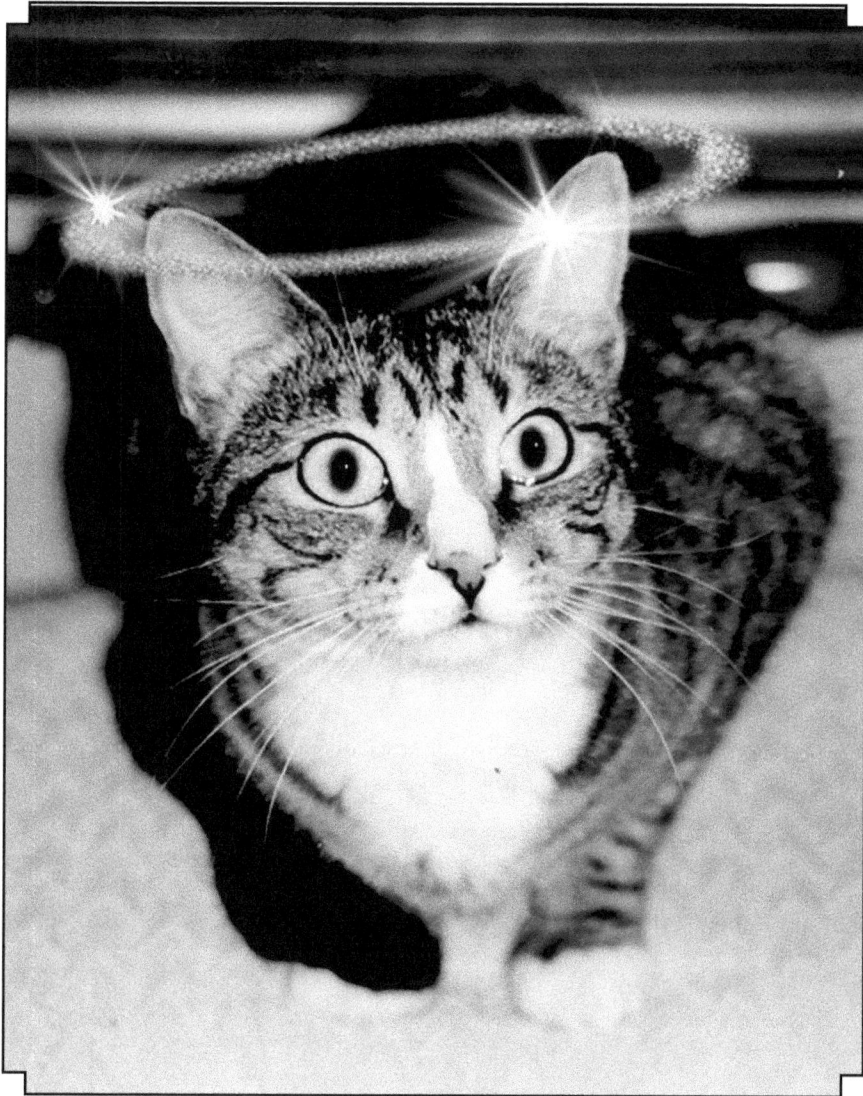

Dot imaged in her alternate universe

Chapter 4: Jan. 1999, In the Wild

We weren't the only ones grieving Dot's loss. My mother, Dorothy (Ma), was crushed to hear her favorite lap warmer was no more. After Gilly, Dot and Kozmo had become an intimate part of our family, and Ma had considered them her "grandkits." When they were near, she fussed over them liberally, using her gentle falsetto kit-speak. She had grown up in the 1920s on a farm in southwest Iowa, where riding cows in the pasture was her favorite pastime. It was probably there that she developed her innate ability to form bonds with animals of all kinds.

Ma and triplet sister Doris with her family's horses

One of Ma's most cherished responsibilities was the task of kit-sitting while we were on business trips or vacations. I was pleased our kitties could experience the same caring environment I had known when growing up in my parents' home. The cats were always happy to see her, and they were returned to us a few ounces heavier and more apt to make eye contact. After all, Ma had many face-to-face disciplining confrontations, especially with her most challenging guest. She never tattled on Kozmo's bad behavior, as she was his trusted friend and confidante, but we knew all too well what she was dealing with.

Shortly after Dot's demise, we left for a business trip to Washington, D.C. This was the first time we had left Kozmo with Ma without his lifelong roomie. Even with his adoring Grandma at his beck and call, the lower two feet of her house were too quiet for his taste.

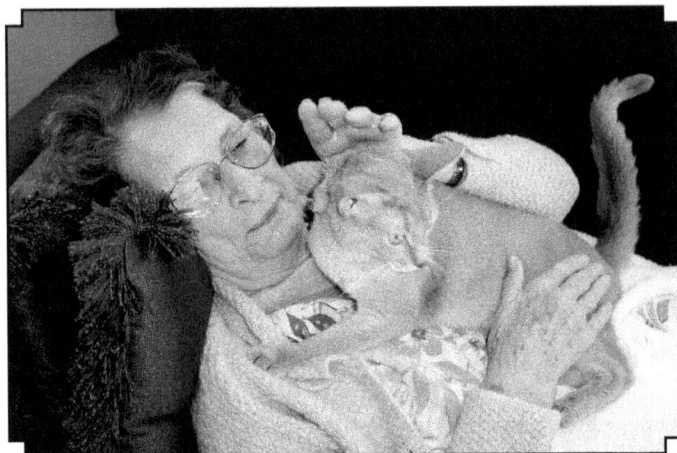
Ma and Kozmo bonding

Jim and I began our journey on a Saturday, enjoying an afternoon of sightseeing in our nation's capital before being surrounded by "suits" for the week of business meetings ahead. As a conscientious daughter of a mother in her eighties, a call to Ma was part of my evening ritual no matter where I was in the world, so that evening I rang her.

When she picked up the phone, I knew immediately by the sound of her voice that something was terribly wrong. Kozmo had disappeared. She claimed she had searched the entire three-story house several times and had found no trace of him. She said she had even gotten the step ladder out of the detached garage and taken it to the basement so she could search each of the exposed rafters. Kozmo was known to inhabit them when he wanted to play "hide-and-seek-the-rascal." Her voice was frantic and breathless, giving away her urgency and escalating her anxiety about possibly losing our fuzzy pal.

Both Jim and I tried to convince her that he had to be somewhere in the house and that she should go to bed, leaving out a small bowl of cat caviar (tuna) to seduce him into giving up on his cruel game. To Ma, this sounded like a sure way to get him to make an appearance, since she had used this con many times before.

I hung up, and Jim and I silently looked at each other. After about ten words of discussion, Jim picked up the telephone to determine what it would cost us to rebook our plane tickets and fly home the following day. Our worst worry was that, in searching for Koz, Ma would end up falling off the ladder, having a heart attack, or falling victim to some other scamp-induced tragedy. We put two plane tickets on hold and went to bed with the intention of checking with Ma early in the morning to see if Kozmo had appeared during the night. If not, we were going to call our business colleagues to cover our conference duties and fly to Ma's house to add four more eyes to the search for our wee fuzzy friend.

As you can guess, we were aboard an airplane headed west come morning. Our onboard conversation consisted of going through every conceivable scenario, trying to outline our plan of attack to find Kozmo. The thought of losing another beloved pet just weeks from the last was unacceptable.

Upon arriving at Ma's, flashlights in hand, we three set off on the same room-to-room search that Ma had done many times before, coming up with the same results. It was then that Ma was put on the hot seat and mercilessly asked to retrace her actions from the previous day. This was of no help.

While sitting in the living room, beginning to lose hope of Kozmo being found healthy, Ma heard the mailman put letters in her mailbox on the front porch. Following her normal routine, she opened the door to retrieve the mail. We watched as the screen door swung back very slowly behind her. Jim's eyes locked with mine as we both realized Kozmo must have gotten outside by following Ma out the day before. Since her eyesight was poor and her view likely over his little head, she must not have realized Koz had followed her out but not back in.

It was January in the Midwest, and the fringes of the yard were heaped with piles of shoveled snow. The midday temperature was in the low twenties, and, if Kozmo was outdoors, he had been through a subzero night. We all pulled on our winter coats, hurried outside, and started calling his name while circling the house, hoping that, if he was out, he would intuitively stay close to where he had last felt warmth. Jim and I set out in opposite directions around the house to save time.

It didn't help our search efforts that, although Kozmo was a rapscallion in every sense of the word, he was virtually mute unless trodden upon. He had been known to lie patiently within closed closets or bedrooms for hours until someone just happened to find him, showing absolutely no concern for the lack of food, water, or bathroom facilities during his imprisonment. I futilely called his name, but didn't hear any type of feline reply, only the identical calls from Jim and Ma at the other sides of the house.

As I rounded the side of the front porch, I noticed there was a freshly-dug depression at the base of its lattice skirting. Upon seeing it, I first thought it was the work of desperate rabbits in search of a place to gain winter shelter, but the critter furrow was too suspicious to bypass without closer investigation.

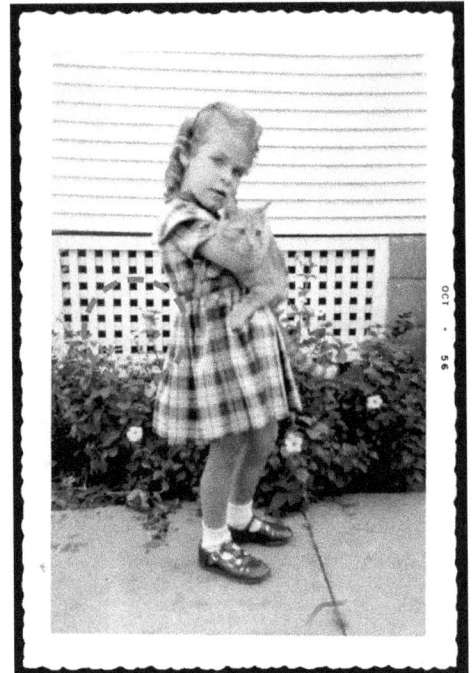

Karen and George. Kozmo's location is highlighted on the left.

I brushed aside some shriveled vegetation lodged against the lattice and squatted down by the enclosed crawl space beneath the porch. I aimed my flashlight through one of the square openings, and, lo and behold, reflected in the beam of light were the shiny, black, saucer-sized eyes of our precious Kozmo.

Little did I realize, in the act of writing the preface of this chapter, that the very photo I'd used to document my initial interaction with felines in 1956 also foretold the exact location Kozmo would choose to hole up to save his life, hoping for our rescue.

Koz immediately wriggled his way under the lattice and into my outstretched arms. He looked as bewildered as Ma, Jim, and I felt, all hoping for the best outcome but fearing the worst. Our reunion was well worth the cost to careers and wallets.

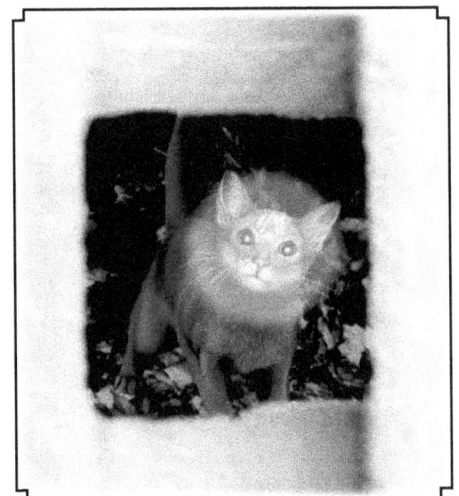

Kozmo under the porch illuminated by the flashlight

Koz had survived his overnight stay alongside

the Grim Reaper with only short-term side effects. The tips of his ears, tail, and foot pads were edged with black fringes of frostbite, and he reeked of motor oil. We thought maybe he had been hugging a warm street-side car engine overnight, which cats are known to do in dire heat-seeking circumstances.

We wrapped him in a warm blanket and, after making sure Ma had recovered from her own frantic day in hell, we got in our car and drove the hour journey to return Kozmo to his home base.

We then gave him the first warm tubby he had ever experienced, which he was only too happy to take. He sat still as we scrubbed him and dried him with a towel. The next step later became his favorite pastime: the hairdryer blow dry. He enjoyed the blustery warmth so much that it became a daily pleasure. After that heavenly experience, he would sit patiently beside me on the bedroom floor every morning while I dried my hair, waiting his turn with the heated whirlwind. However, his new habit of sitting on or near a heat register during the winter months was a sign he never forgot his harrowing escapade.

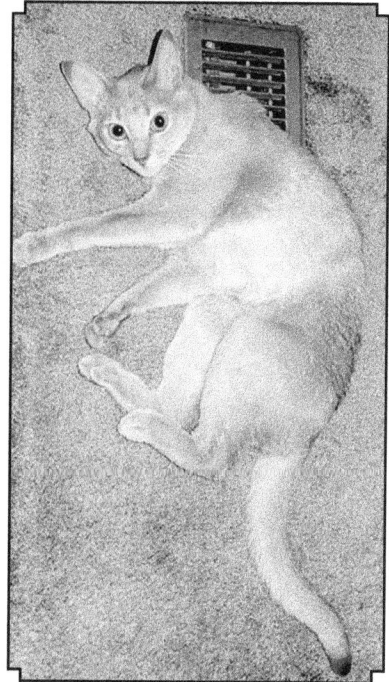

Kozmo with frostbitten extremities

Kozmo getting his daily blowout

Chapter 5: Apr. 2000, BB, King of the Blues

We contacted Kozmo's breeder in hopes of doubling our family fun by adding another Abyssinian to our fold. She told us she was no longer in the kitten supply chain, but knew of a couple who were breeding descendants of her stud in a nearby city. The cat was aptly named "Flyer" due to his oversized ears. We quickly made the contact call and were ecstatic to find there was a new batch of nearly-weaned kittens awaiting new parents. We were in the car and on the road in minutes.

Upon walking in the front door of Flyer's progenies' house, our ankles were enveloped by a passel of tiny, multicolored fluff balls. It was like finding ourselves transported to the Star Trek episode "The Trouble with Tribbles" and similar to being in the eye of a happiness hurricane.

There was one bristly, gray imp that caught our attention immediately. He was the busiest of the bunch and fearlessly broke from the pack. He craned his neck to make eye contact, then cocked it, as if mulling over his own decision of approval. Oh, that all-important, two-way, deal-sealing eye contact. Our hearts were once again taken by storm.

BB stands out from the crowd

We watched the breeder and his partner prepare our pet carrier with provisions for our new addition to the family during his hour-long ride to his new home. There was a cuddly blanket, a bowl of water, some kibble, and a small aluminum foil pie plate filled with litter. We loaded our little chum into the back seat of the car and hit the road.

About ten minutes into the ride, we were overcome by a foul stench that made our eyes water. I looked in the back seat and, sure enough, the little dude had poop-a-dooped in his litter plate. Jim was wildly searching through burning tears for a place to pull over and get out of the car as fast as possible. Thankfully, there was a McDonald's ahead. We certainly had no appetite for food, but we spotted an outdoor trashcan that would be a perfect place to make a quick deposit. As young as he was, our wee pal managed to keep all of his offering neatly within the bounds of the pie plate. With quick and careful extractions of the wee kitten and his latest creation, we dumped the waste and kept the prize, putting him back in his carrier, much to his relief. He curled up nose to tail and fell asleep in seconds.

Back on the road, our conversation switched to the memory of Kozmo presenting us with a similar gift the first day he was welcomed into our home. Maybe this curious ritual was an innate Abyssinian behavior, based somewhere in their ancient Ethiopian background. Then again, maybe it was just the normal feline digestion process coupled with a natural instinct to void wherever and whenever they have the urge, especially if there was an absorbent, granular substance nearby. Having so far chronicled every event in Kozmo's life as significant, it was easy for me to interpret all acts of our beloved pets as predestined, so this initial behavior in our kitten was really no surprise.

Once home, it was time to offer up our solution to Kozmo's quest for a suitable Dot replacement. The pet carrier was placed on the floor in our family room, just as it had been when Kozmo first touched his own tiny paws to the nap of foreign carpeting. Our new kitten merrily sauntered out of the carrier, spinning his tiny head to take in his new surroundings. Understandably, his new brother had quite a different reaction.

It was impossible to photograph the expressions of the pair when they first set eyes upon each other. However, these photos were taken very close to the time of the event. I would best describe Kozmo's reaction as utter disbelief. He proceeded to give the foreigner a wide berth as he estimated the wee one's superpowers.

Meanwhile, the selection of another appropriate pet name was underway. The kitten was a purebred Abyssinian with a coat of slate-blue banded ticking offset with warm beige. After substantial mulling and culling, we agreed upon "BB," a simple description for whom we felt would become "The King of the Blues," like the singer BB King. After all, his official breed was "Blue Abyssinian." We also decided our preferred nickname for him would be BB Crapper, for obvious reasons, but we ultimately shortened that to "Beeb."

Beeb's facial features were totally minimized by his flaring ears. To fully understand the spatial dominance of his aural appendages, a scientific investigation was undertaken here, using crude photographic scaling.

BB sees Kozmo

Kozmo sees BB

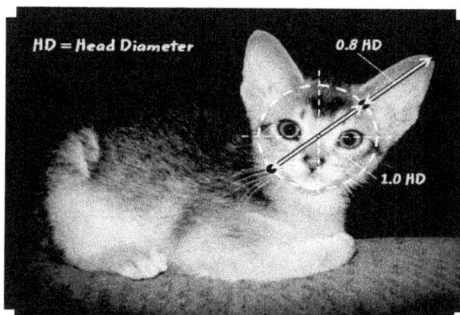

Scaling of BB's ears relative to his head

His hearing was very sensitive, and he could spin those triangular soundwave receivers around almost backwards, enabling him to pick up the slightest peep anywhere in the house.

The dimensional disproportion of Beeb's body parts was somewhat comical and deserves a distinctive caricature drawing to further highlight the contrasts.

Beeb was ten weeks old upon arrival, very teeny and nearly weightless. It was hard to tell if he was actually in your hands when cuddling him. As he wandered around, exploring his new environment and taking his itty-bitty steps, he looked like a bristly bug on the floor.

He seemed totally fearless. He came directly to each of us, but would squirt from our grasp as soon as he could to curl in a ball and roll on the floor just beyond our reach.

On this day of introductions, Kozmo was in heightened alarm mode. As Beeb self-confidently approached him over and over, Koz would cower and walk backwards to maintain a consistent three-foot distance. Beeb would follow his new roomie faithfully, no matter what the physical challenge. As Kozmo broke for the litter box in the basement, his student quickly shadowed behind, undaunted by the carpeted steps that were taller than he was. It was readily apparent that Beeb had been trained on stairs back at his previous home, since he made quick but

Baby Beeb

somewhat clumsy work of them. We tailed the pair to make sure there were no unsupervised kerfuffles on the lower floor. To our amazement, we found Kozmo standing beside one of two litter boxes we had prepared, watching his little brother taking care of his business. How had the teensy guy scaled that slippery, high wall of the litter box? Had Kozmo given him a boost? We were so pleased that Beeb already knew the all-important rules of feline hygiene (especially after the unexpected event during our car ride) that we ignored our questions of "how" it happened and mentally checked the major hurdle of potty training off the pet parent to-do list.

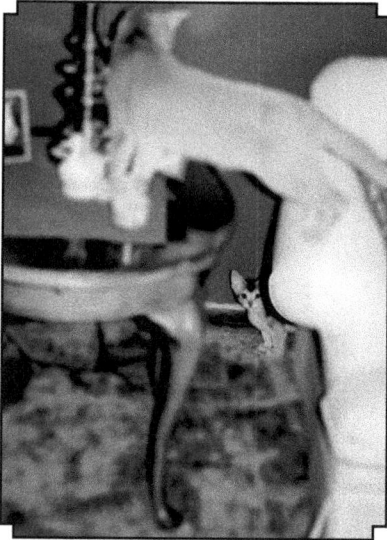

Kozmo balancing over BB
at the baseboard

Kozmo took a full week to adapt to and fully accept his compadre. Each day, the cordon radius would decrease, but Koz was still very cautious. When the Beeb was near, Kozzie's two golden eyes were always narrowed on him.

It was on the eighth day of their cohabitation that Kozmo finally walked up to Beeb and started licking off those spikey bristles in his baby brother's coat, still present from his pre-weaned days with his grimy littermates. Once thoroughly tongue-raked by a trained professional, Beeb was warmly accepted by his older bro.

The three-foot cordon narrows

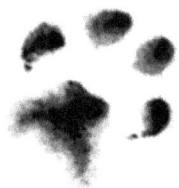

Chapter 6: May 2000–Sept. 2002, Brutha from Anutha Mutha

Early on, the Beeb's acceptance into our tribe resulted in a fairly even balance of power among family players, primarily because Kozmo was totally off-balance. Being a brother was not in Kozmo's gamut of practiced behaviors. The sudden presence of a clingy half-pint usurping available pet parent adoration harshed his mellow, to put it mildly.

Kozmo below his shadow

Beeb was so close to his new bro that it was hard to tell if he was Kozzie's shadow or an additional skin layer. A lot of piggyback play was demonstrated by the two, bringing to mind Kozmo's own early "yeehaw" days with his sister, Dot. However, this time Beeb was in the saddle and Koz was the bronco to be busted. Coincidence or karma? Confirmation that what goes around comes around.

As the early weeks of bro-hood played out, the camaraderie between the boys solidified. Intense cuddling ensued, allowing Kozmo to subtly pass on his meticulous grooming practices to his baby brutha. There were multiple training sessions, some ending with a sharp paw bop to the top of Beeb's head, marking Koz's frustration with his novice's lack of attention to detail. How were those giant gray ears to get spotless without concentration on the task at hand?

Kozmo grooming BB

BB grooming Kozmo

As he traipsed through adolescence, Beeb slowly began to fill out. He took on a shape similar to his father, a strong-shanked specimen of the Abyssinian breed. Unfortunately, BB had short front legs and long back legs, giving the appearance of always walking downhill. True, this was not a desirable trait for a show cat, but we knew he was destined solely for home posing performances. We thought his asymmetrical stance and oversized ears were a large part of his offbeat charm.

Perhaps Kozmo's tutelage was taken too seriously by the Beeb. He began grooming his belly so thoroughly he cropped the hair completely off, leaving his delicate, pink underbelly exposed. It was my favorite spot to massage him when he was seated on my lap. His tummy was silky and warm. This ritual instantly put both of us at ease. He would look me in the eyes and purr notes which I was sure meant, "Please don't stop."

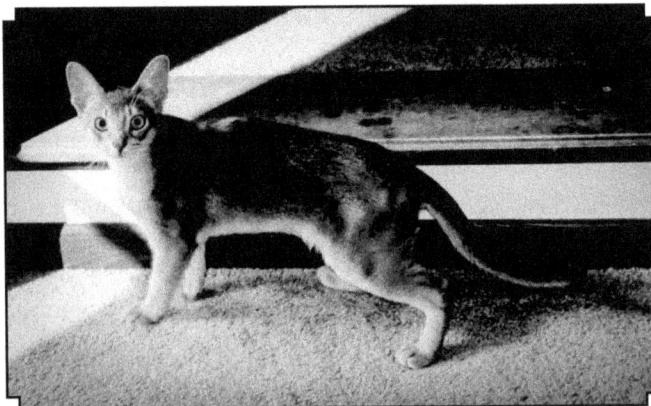

Asymmetrical Proportions

BB was a Kozmo fanatic, just like us. We spent most of our downtime watching Koz's antics as our primary source of entertainment. However, a short time after BB's adoption, we purchased our first large-screen, high-definition television. Initially, there were just a few broadcast stations taking advantage of the crystal clear, vibrant screen quality, so, to marvel at the new technology, we started watching more documentary channels like Discovery, which included many programs on wildlife.

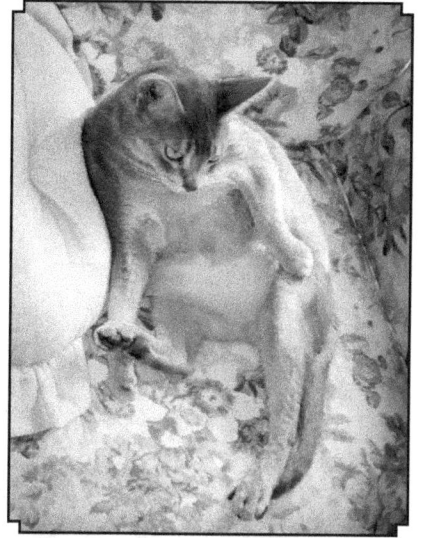
BB overgrooms his belly

The Beeb was mesmerized by nature on the screen, especially mammals, fish, and insects.

To separate him from the screen at night, we had to change channels or turn the TV off. He would then slowly turn and trudge out of the room. He was a deep thinker and had only just begun to add wrinkles to his gray matter by analyzing his own psyche and surroundings. Although the same breed, he was clearly cut from a different cloth than Kozmo.

BB marvels at elephants on HDTV

Beeb's absolute favorite program was the *Sunrise Earth* series on *Discovery*, consisting of an hour-long presentation of dawn in exotic locations around the world. He could swim underwater with the manatees in Florida, touch the wings of a butterfly along the Amazon, or swirl in Maine's Kidney Pond with a baby moose. BB enjoyed the soundtrack provided by the cast of animals, which made it even more authentic.

It wasn't long before the student became the teacher and Koz was beside his baby brother, jostling to get the prime vantage point for virtual stalking. BB occasionally had to settle for the smaller TV screens within his realm to get his video fix.

BB slowly expanded his interests to all sorts of TV genres. He became obsessed with commercials and local and global news channels. Often, the nightly news would include random animal stories at the end of broadcasts to lighten the audience's mood after hearing the sorrows of the day. Beeb would wait patiently, becoming totally fixated on the screen when he caught sight of his preferred video topics.

I distinctly remember him watching a story about myotonic baby goats that fainted when startled. He was so engrossed by the story that, when it was over, he jumped to the TV stand and looked behind the set to see where the tiny goats had gone. He clearly needed to know more, but was sadly disappointed when the little kids were nowhere to be found.

Kozmo lovingly introduced BB to all of his own favorite pastimes, further broadening the little guy's horizons. At the top of the list was reveling in the Fourth of July Independence Day hubbub. Koz was always tipped off that the holiday was near when he heard and felt occasional window-shaking blasts set off by our scofflaw neighbors a week prior to the official celebration. We provided Koz his own legal fireworks show every year on the backyard patio. He loved Roman candles and flame-throwing tanks. The Beeb figured that if Kozmo thought it was great, then he did, too, although he looked a bit more wary, as if he was not quite sold on the idea.

Halloween was another lollapalooza. At that time of year, Kozmo loved to hear the doorbell, which signaled incoming strangers of the wee kind. Trick-or-treaters would squeal with delight when they saw the cats tumbling over themselves to be the first to get to the door, and the kids would beg to touch them. The kits would step out onto the porch and into wildly petting hands and questions from the tots about the boys' furry lifestyle. Even after the doorbell quit ringing, the fuzz-wuzzies took positions by the window, eyes peeled for any stray ghouls or goblins. One Halloween per year was just not enough.

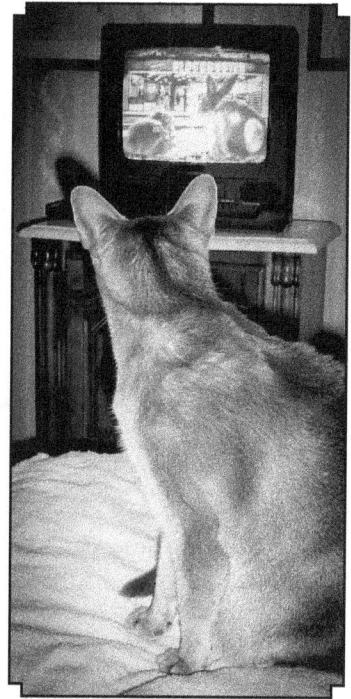

BB feeding his obsession with animals on TV

Koz and BB celebrate the Fourth of July

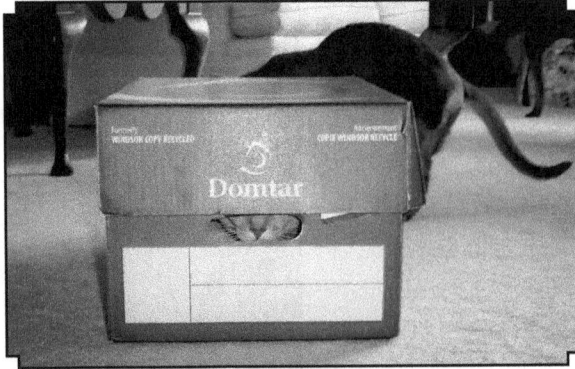

Kozmo and Beeb became the best of friends and were perfectly matched playmates. Koz was constantly in need of a willing foil or collaborator, and BB was always near to fit the bill. Household items were used as props to add elements of complexity to ordinary feline wiles, such as "Kitty in a Box."

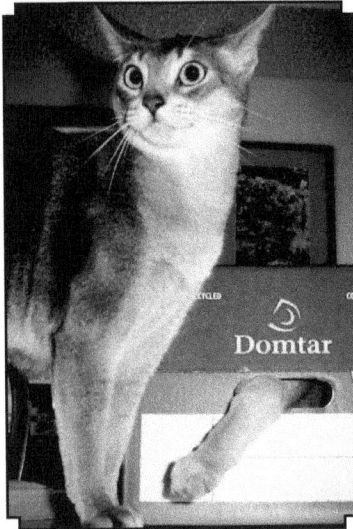

Every room in our house was filled with stashes of cat toys to keep the boys from getting bored. Some needed to be animated by means of a bystander, such as the classic Puncharoo hand puppet from the Seattle-based novelty store Archie McPhee. Koz and BB loved to bob and weave away from the flurry of jabs and startling uppercuts that the 'Roo could throw at them. Some punches hit pay dirt, but not many.

PUNCHEROO

Twist tie

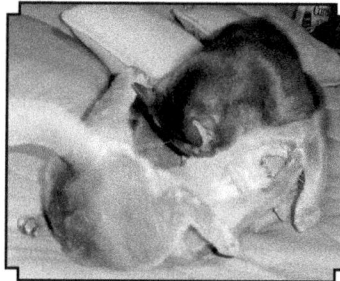

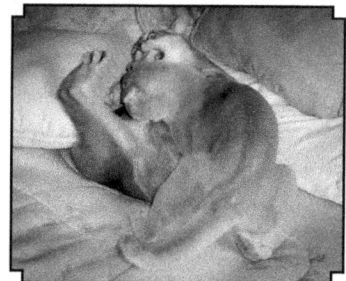

Even something as simple as a crinkled twist tie could be a source of stiff competition between the bros. Although both cats were lightning fast when it came to batting things around like a hockey puck, BB was the champ of this sport, often daring his "br-ival" to snatch his quarry.

Sometimes a scuffle arose, and it was hard to tell the difference between protagonist and antagonist, roles which they seemed to switch at random.

The ultimate display of brudderly love occurred when we were away from the house on a day trip, leaving Kozmo and BB without supervision. Unknowingly, we had left the house with the Beeb shut on the wrong side of the master bedroom door. When we arrived home late in the evening, we were met by an anxious Kozmo, sitting on what we termed the 'worry stair,' closest he could get to the garage. We barely had the door open a crack when we saw his nose poke out. As we opened the door all the way, he turned tail and ran up the stairs in a blur. This did not bode well. Something was amiss.

We followed him through the house and were stunned by the sight we found at the closed door of our bedroom. There were handfuls of cat toys strewn around the base of the door. Some were lying under it, partially obscured from view. We opened the door, and there we found the other part of the puzzle. BB was sitting calmly, staring up at us with his round, copper-colored eyes. He didn't seem the least bit stressed or even anxious to get to the litter box. We were suddenly swished by Kozmo as he brushed by us to get to his little, abandoned buddy. They swirled around each other, touching noses multiple times to check and double-check ID's, and then they were off down the hall toward their next adventure.

How would Sherlock Holmes have deduced what had occurred on this day of feline anguish? We surveyed the scene, looking for clues as to what had happened while we were gone. First, we checked the cat toy caches around the house to find the source of the bootie. Sure enough, the small kitchen drawer reserved for "boys-only" was fully open and lacking many of its usual suspects. Although we didn't have a surveillance tape to confirm our deduction, we knew the thief had to be Kozmo, since he was the only one with access to the drawer.

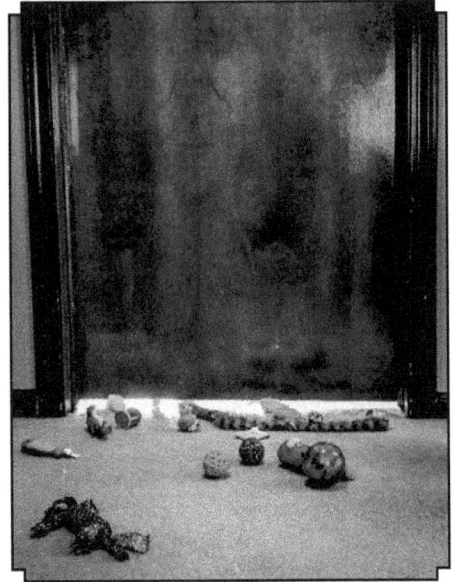
Cat toy field outside bedroom door

Koz had a history of being caught "red-pawed" in the past, and was known to jump on the kitchen counter, open the toy drawer, and pick his latest crush from the selection available. We envisioned Koz panicking once he realized he was cut off from his baby bro. No doubt the two normally silent siblings pawed distress signals beneath the closed door to assess their situation and determine the best coping mechanism for dealing with their previously unexperienced separation.

BB seeing Kozmo under the door

We believed Kozmo then went down to the drawer, opened it, pulled BB's favorites out one by one, and hauled them individually to the bedroom door. There was definite evidence that Beeb had tried to pull the toys he could reach into his prison, but, without claws, he couldn't manage to pull them totally under the door. Curses!

Kozmo seeing BB under the door

Like many animal lovers, we had projected human characteristics onto our beloved boys early on in their lives, as documented in this mewlogy. The purpose was to entertain ourselves, but also to see which of us could come up with the more outlandish commentary on what our pets were thinking as they went about their normal day. This particular incident, however, was beyond even our own silly imaginations.

As we told our friends and family about the unprecedented event, we were met with skepticism, though there was a small minority who took us at our word. Two of them were our respective mothers. Always the first question out of their mouths upon seeing us in person was "How are the cats?" or "What did the cats do today?" They listened to our recap, their faces giving away their multiple emotions as the tale got more and more inconceivable. In addition, they both related our blow-by-blow report to their own pet-loving inner circle of friends, glad to have something to talk about besides their ailments and the weather.

The only other person who took us seriously was our softhearted, impish friend Lolo. She enjoyed the story so much that she wrote her own interpretation of it and read it to her three young nieces, who begged for more details when she was done. It was Lolo who encouraged me to share the escapades of our resourceful kit-cats, which earned her a spot on the dedication page.

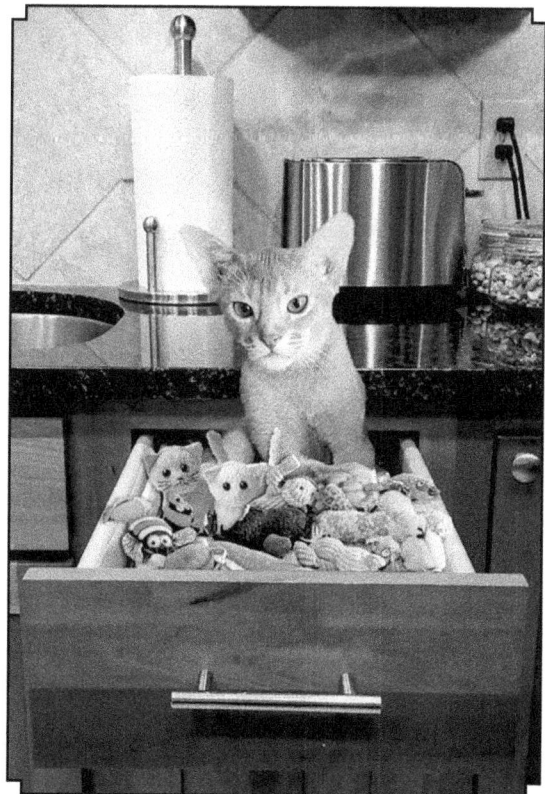

Kozmo looking for BB's favorites in the kitchen toy drawer

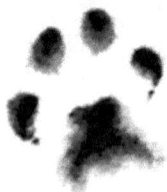

As you would expect, my mother Dorothy's petsitting responsibilities were rescinded in January 1999 after Kozmo's unexpected overnight field trip in freezing temperatures. Ma was perfectly willing to relinquish those duties, since she doubted her own ability to keep Kozmo properly shepherded. With the addition of Beeb to our herd, we all agreed it was necessary to assign custodial duties to a more adept warden when Jim and I were away.

However, Ma remained a doting granny when she came to visit us. Since she wasn't a permanent member of our household, each reunion began with a short, mad scramble to corral the mewlings, followed by tight, swaddling squeezes to calm their nerves. Once they realized she was a familiar friend and not a fiendish foe, they relaxed and welcomed her flattering praise and loving pats.

In October 2002, Ma experienced a decline in health. The cats helped her to make a smooth emotional transition from life on her own an hour's drive away to one in an assisted living facility just a mile from our house. Although she would have preferred to keep her independence and remain by herself, she realized it was time for more help from her loved ones and knowledgeable healthcare professionals.

Mother and daughter corralling the kitties

we could then have daily visits at her apartment instead of weekly ones at her past home. She saw the boys more than she ever had before and relished every minute of their company. At the age of eighty-six, she was interacting with people more than she had for several years and adapted to it fairly well, considering her introverted personality.

Early in the morning, on the day of her eighty-seventh birthday, Ma fell in her bedroom while getting dressed. By the time I reached her apartment, she was already on the first responders' gurney, who were shuttling her out of her room. She was so glad to see a familiar face among all the strangers around her and immediately relaxed, telling me what happened as they wheeled her to the ambulance.

I met her at the emergency room, where they x-rayed her and found she had broken her hip. This was a common occurrence for someone her age, and, due to her reasonably good physical health, she was expected to withstand the required hip joint replacement surgery needed to fix the problem. However, I knew it would be a challenge for me to ensure that her recovery process followed the principles of her strongly-held religious beliefs.

Her Christian faith followed a literal interpretation of the apostle Luke's urgings in Acts 15:29: "You are to abstain from food sacrificed to idols, from blood," and other things. She believed this verse, along with others in the Bible, prohibited her from accepting blood transfusions, no matter how dire the circumstance. She had made it clear to me when I became a young adult that she wished me to respect this belief without fail and asked me to be her advocate if she was ever incapacitated. She even had a card in her billfold with her signature demanding the right to dictate her destiny with respect to this type of medical treatment. She also had a living will that specified her life not be maintained by artificial means if she was not expected to recover from a life-threatening ailment. We had discussed her final wishes many times in detail, and I had no doubt what was expected of me at the end of her life.

Surprisingly, it was fairly easy to find a surgeon who would perform her procedure without using any blood products, since there were many other patients with similar beliefs. We were both very relieved. The operation went smoothly, and she awoke from her spinal anesthetic giggling, marveling at the fact she couldn't feel anything in the lower part of her body at first.

A day after her surgery, however, she developed a fever and gradually became incoherent. A hole had somehow formed in the wall of her intestine, and she had to have part of it removed and repaired to prevent her death. This required she be fully sedated and put on a ventilator. Her new doctor was also well-practiced in bloodless surgical procedures, and another possible religious conflict was successfully dodged.

The two surgeries resulted in relatively minor blood loss, but she was kept in the intensive care ward and sedated to minimize her movements. This kept her intravenous needle connections to healing medications and fluids stabilized, but, while adjusting her bedding, a nurse unintentionally loosened her port, and Ma began to bleed profusely from the puncture wound as I helplessly watched, screaming for help from her bedside. A flock of nurses were able to stem the bleeding, but not soon enough to prevent a massive loss of her precious lifeblood.

While at her bedside, the hospital chaplain came to talk to me about her situation. When I explained to him what my promise to her had been, he surprisingly agreed with my intentions. Though he was not of her faith, he knew its principles and understood the critical importance of following her beliefs to her last breath. He then went directly to the nurses' station and explained to them the need for me to support my mother's wishes when she wasn't able. He also talked to all of Ma's doctors to make it clear I wouldn't be changing my decision, just as she would never have changed hers.

Ten days after her admission to the hospital, the doctor stopped her ventilator to see if she could breathe on her own. She could not, and her breathing support system was resumed.

I then called her close friend, an elder from her congregation who had been coaching me through the religious choices I was making for her, and asked if he could come to give her whatever form of last rites were applicable. He made the trip from her hometown immediately. When he arrived, he spoke softly in her ear at her bedside, then remained as the doctor removed her breathing tube.

Our expectations were that she would pass quickly, but she continued her labored breathing for over an hour. The doctor confirmed that her chances for recovery from the cascading events of her current condition at the age of eighty-seven years were nil. We arranged for a hospice room on the upper floor of the hospital so that Jim and I were able to be with her around the clock.

It was time for us to be there for the woman I fell in love with the moment I saw her. She was the most loving, trusting, trustworthy, funny, capable life guide a person could wish for, and she would always be part of me. She was my best friend and confidante from the beginning of my days.

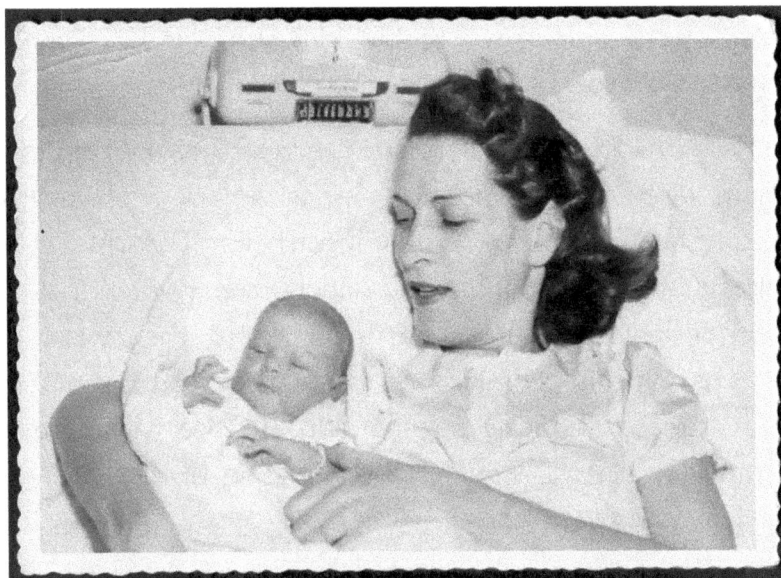

Me and my bestie on our first day together

I had always dreaded my vow to be Ma's advocate, but the probability of me making final judgment was low, so I never dwelt on it. It remains the most difficult thing I've ever endured, even given her specific instructions on how to proceed.

I reflected upon my experience, shared with Jim, of choosing the fate of Ma's feline namesake, Dot, and with her own life-and-death dilemma. There was a wide difference in intensity between the loss of my family member and that of my pet, but both held concern for the comfort of each failing life in common. Overcoming grief and focusing on the empathetic action to be taken was of highest priority.

I remembered the tearful day of Dot's last visit to the veterinarian. She was lying so weak and frail on the examining table, peacefully waiting for her own transition. I was so glad I had that personal experience with her to reflect upon. It had been a practice session of extreme loss, met in person, without any veiled interface to block the anguish. Though she was an animal, she was as dear to me as a family member, always glad to see me, comforting my woes and lightening my burdens. After Dot's death, I realized I would have to face similar situations of painful loss and would have to come to terms with the fact that her welcoming life force would be forever missing. It had been a blessing in disguise. I learned to welcome and dwell on pictures and memories of her, always thankful to have shared the pleasant and even the challenging days we lived through together.

Three days after entering her hospice room, Ma took her last breath. Both Jim and I were by her side. After all of the arduous breaths she had taken for those final few days, her last was long and relaxed, fading away to silence. A mere two weeks earlier we had been cuddling kitties side by side, laughing and joking. Now there was a vacancy in my soul, already waiting to be patched with thoughts of her and a plan of how to fill it, thanks to the previous death of our beloved Dot.

It was after Ma's loss that I felt inspired by my experiences to pass this newfound knowledge on to others. I intended to write a book called *The Key to Freedom*. The book was going to use human-like animals as main characters in a humorous, encouraging story about developing the emotional forbearance necessary to deal with the harsh realities of life. My most difficult lifetime experience – enabling my mother's death – was to be my inspiration in encouraging others to grieve with healing results in mind, since the anguish of this time was similar to the emotional distress of euthanizing my cherished pet.

Those of us who have already lost that extraordinary person or animal know the sorrow involved in tolerating the mournful void left for us. We also have the need to commiserate with others about the passing of that special human (or moggy) and move forward, with only memories to cope. My envisioned book was intended to fill the need for a simple, soulful expression of empathy, a visually compelling reference and keepsake that could provide grieving advice, humor, and optimism for those who lament.

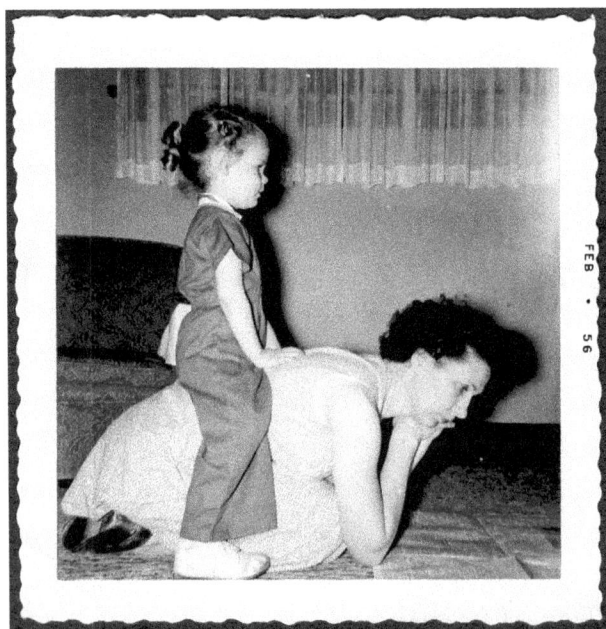

Our own yeehaw moment

Little did I imagine, when I was three years old, sitting atop Ma's back as she read the news-paper, that I would recognize that I had actually been the first character to have the bronco-busting "yeehaw" experience of my extended human/cat family.

Chapter 8: Nov 2003-Sept. 2010, The Key to Freedom

sal·va·tion (sal-vāSH(ə)n) n.

1. Preservation or deliverance from harm, ruin, or loss.

My mother's death marked an emotional low for me, against which all sad experiences were then compared. From that point on, any negative occurrence in my daily activities was compared to her passing and instantly judged to be less significant than originally thought. In that context, bad things were rendered harmless. She had unknowingly gifted me an unexpected sense of freedom. I met challenges with much less fear than I had before. This proved to be a form of salvation for me, as defined above. With that liberty, the assurance that I had followed her wishes to her last breath, and the unconditional love of Jim, Kozmo and the Beeb, I was able to sustain myself and recapture the love of life she had raised me to enjoy.

A couple of months later, during the holidays, Jim handed me a heavy present, about which I remarked "This must be a rock!" It was. A large, smooth river rock about the size of an artisanal bread loaf with the intertwined figures of my loyal pals Kozmo and BB skillfully painted on by our talented neighbor, Jane. It was not only a singular memento, but a solid reminder of processing my loss and successfully managing my grief. Another amazing gift!

Koz and Beeb Pet Rock

With my newly enriched tolerance for the harsh realities of life, I began to write an outline for *The Key to Freedom*. I initially thought it would be a relatively simple endeavor and intended to illustrate it with my own drawings. I chose my cast of characters from animals in our neighborhood with whom I was well acquainted. Of course, the starring roles were to be played by the boys, Kozmo and the Beeb. Their hand-drawn prototypes took me months to complete, but I was happy with how the caricatures finally captured their impish personalities.

The next task was creating eccentric supporting creatures that would flesh out the storyline. I gave Kozmo an unlikely friend who, in the real world, could be his potential victim. I thought a symbiotic relationship with alternating roles of antagonist-protagonist would be interesting for them to explore together. Vlado (*Rattus norvegicus*), a plucky brown rat, materialized. I saw him as Kozmo's most loyal friend, unintimidated by Koz's raucous behavior and forgiving of his sometimes self-serving personality.

Main characters of the Key to Freedom

I realized that BB must also have some close acquaintances. I sifted through my memories for the most intriguing critters I'd crossed paths with and conjured a long-eared mini lop rabbit named Clyde. The real Clyde's primary home was a large pet carrier in the garage of a neighbor who lived about two blocks from us. One evening, during a walk in the bitter cold winter of 2004, Jim and I passed his owner's house and found Clyde grazing on the grassy stubble poking through the snow in his front yard. Although this was an unusual place to find him, we hesitated only a moment to say a few words of greeting, then passed by. Clyde took this acknowledgement as an invitation to join us on our walk. We certainly didn't want to take him away from his home turf, so we started walking faster, which prompted him to hop faster. Then we

Vlado, the Rat

began to run, which caused him to break into a loping sprint. Clearly, we either had to pick him up and take him back to his owner or adopt him. We chose the former as the appropriate choice. This amusing escapade earned him the right to appear in the book.

Lastly, I chose my favorite nearly-neckless, neurotic bird, a white-breasted nuthatch, and called her Fidgety. These birds are renowned for perching upside-down on tree trunks, though they don't always go down. This tendency gives them a very recognizable posture, with their heads craned up and horizontal. Their movements are herky-jerky as they look in all directions, without deference to gravity, pecking limbs in search of insects. Every good story needs edgy characters to stimulate mayhem.

These would be the leading actors of *The Key to Freedom*. A motley crew, indeed, with many innate differences from which to draw substance for a moral tale.

When originally conceived, the audience of the book was to be the broad range of people who are Harry Potter fans (which I consider to be all ages, including mine). With the aid of original illustrations, I hoped to build a framework to make an entertaining yet poignant fantasy world reflecting reality.

Clyde, the Mini Lop

Fidgety, the
White-Breasted Nuthatch

The Cast of Characters:
BB, Kozmo, Vlado, Clyde and Fidgety

This task expanded exponentially as I thought about it more and more, but it was serving its purpose. The creative process allowed me to reflect on the agony of losing my loved ones and place those emotions on paper, putting them in a context that significantly reduced the sting of their effect on my daily life.

The following pages outline the plot of the book.

The Backstory of the Plot
(to be detailed in Chapter 1
of my *The Key to Freedom* manuscript)

Vlado and Kozmo are denizens of a large, ancient, crumbling mansion, which is shared with a husband-wife pair of human curmudgeons. The animals' existence within the manor depends totally on their ability to convince the humans it is infested with vermin.

Periodically, Vlado runs between the legs of the wife in the kitchen, making her scream. Kozmo enters the room (as if in a well-rehearsed play), and grasps the struggling Vlado in his razor-sharp maw. Koz sprints confidently to the door and is released into the wild by the wife, where she assumes he will devour his defenseless prey.

Shortly after duping the wife, Koz trots back to the door, licking his chops, while Vlado hides nearby.

When the door opens, Kozmo enters to a congratulatory pat on the head. As the wife closes the door, turning to get him a food-scrap reward, Vlado flicks around the edge of the entry and runs to the attic.

To ensure their shady lifestyle continues uninterrupted, Koz and Vlado occasionally run frantically in random patterns around the attic (their personal 'hood) as a reminder to those listening below of the cat's essential contribution to the family's wellbeing. The supportive relationship between the two scammers results in a trusting and mutually enjoyable bond.

One day, while performing their practiced chase scene in the attic, Kozmo loses his grip on the slippery timber floor and slides into a narrow, seemingly bottomless gap between the interior and exterior walls of the manor. Vlado witnesses the sudden disappearance of his companion and dashes to the ledge where the darkness swallowed his buddy and looks down, into the void. As Vlado's eyes slowly adjust to the shadowy depth before him, he starts to make out the crumpled shape of his feline cohort far, far below.

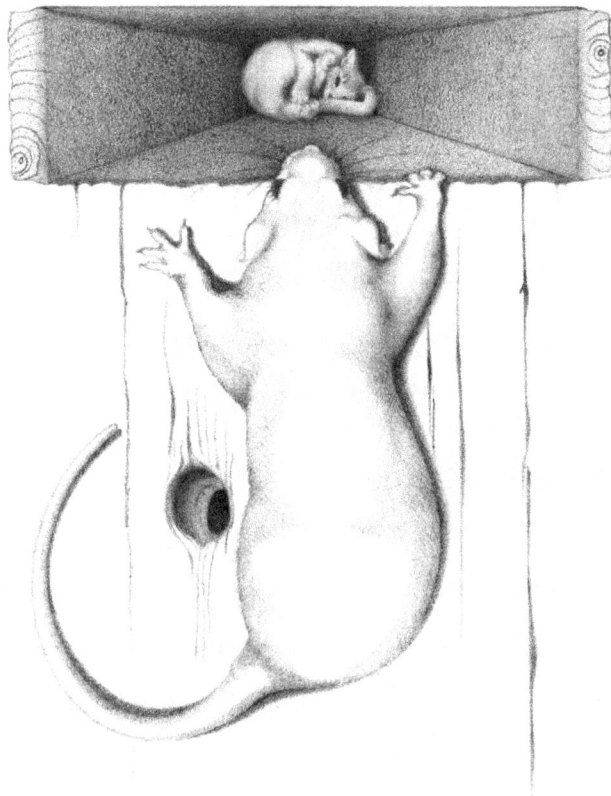

Vlado looks at Kozmo trapped within the wall joists

There isn't a sound, not even the faintest breath or other sign of life. Vlado's mind is spinning in fear for Kozmo's fate. He turns and runs to one of the two windows at each end of the long attic dormer. His eyes desperately search the grounds for a source of help that is not there.

Vlado frantically looks for help

Vlado turns and races back to hang his head over the ledge again, hoping to see a more hopeful image of his dearest friend.

The plot background ends here.
The first page of the actual manuscript follows.

Chapter 1: The Key to Freedom
Against the Wall

Am I Dead?

The shriek was deafening. Had Kozmo actually uttered the sound? For that matter, was there even proof of a consciousness generating this scenario?

Now all was darkness, a void made solid by the weighty pressure of silence. He shuddered and asked again, "Am I dead?" This time it was but a whisper, not formed in Kozmo's thoughts, but as a guttural, forced emission from lungs lean on nourishment:"Nghahhhhh…."

Can I see? This was definitely intentional thought, not spoken word, for he was beginning to regain connection to his senses. As the reflection thickened, he felt his lids in motion, felt them stretching long and wide with the intensity of his searching gaze. The void again, but this time flecked with swirling bits. His hunt for reality continued, anxious at first, then frantic, in pursuit of the slightest recognizable image.

Then he saw them. Tiny specks of white, flashing without rhythm, blurry and circling. As Kozmo squinted to reduce his frenzied field of view, the circling stopped and the blurs began to clear. There were two of them now. The relief of mentally reaching out and connecting with something in this anchorless universe was calming to him. He inhaled slowly and tried to exhale without fear of losing the last bit of his fragile life force. His breath was becoming surprisingly steady. Then, suddenly, he made a connection with the twin points of light and felt relief wash over him. They were the eyes of his trusted companion Vlado, reflecting the muted light from the attic windows.

Looking for page two of the manuscript? As of this moment, there is no page two, nor page three.

Due to overwhelming career demands, *The Key to Freedom* had to be put on a back burner, just as I had finally started writing the actual story. I would never have guessed it would be thirteen years before I would have the opportunity to pick it up again.

When I was on the eve of retirement, I suffered an unusual pain in my abdomen and was taken to the hospital's emergency room. After two days of fruitless searching for causes, exploratory surgery discovered an internal hernia that had pinched off half of my upper intestine, causing its tissue to die within me. Before, during, or after the procedure to remove the useless part of my intestine, I suffered a hemorrhagic stroke. After six months of intense rehabilitation, I retired from the job I could no longer perform. My neuropsychologist suggested I focus my waking efforts on something I enjoyed, that would continue to stimulate my impaired neural circuits. This mewlogy was waiting patiently for me to continue, the perfect therapy for relearning things that now needed to be accessed via circuitous synapse routes. In order to have any hope of sharing this story before my ashes were one with the universe, I modified my original plan.

I reorganized my *Mewlogy* outline, deciding to create a short, inexpensive book which could also serve as a sort of multipage sympathy card. I decided it would take the form of a journal, aimed at cat aficionados who have lost a loving feline, recently or in the past. If, when in print, this mewlogy generates a profit, half will be given to local animal shelters, full of felines patiently waiting to be a Kozmo or a BB for another lucky family.

Hopefully, this story will temporarily fill the void of loss and the burden of heartache with welcome optimism, if just for a moment.

Chapter 9: Oct. 2004-Oct. 2010, Living Large

Our middle-aged years were made complete by sharing them with the middle-aged years of our favorite fun-loving fuzzballs, Kozmo and BB.

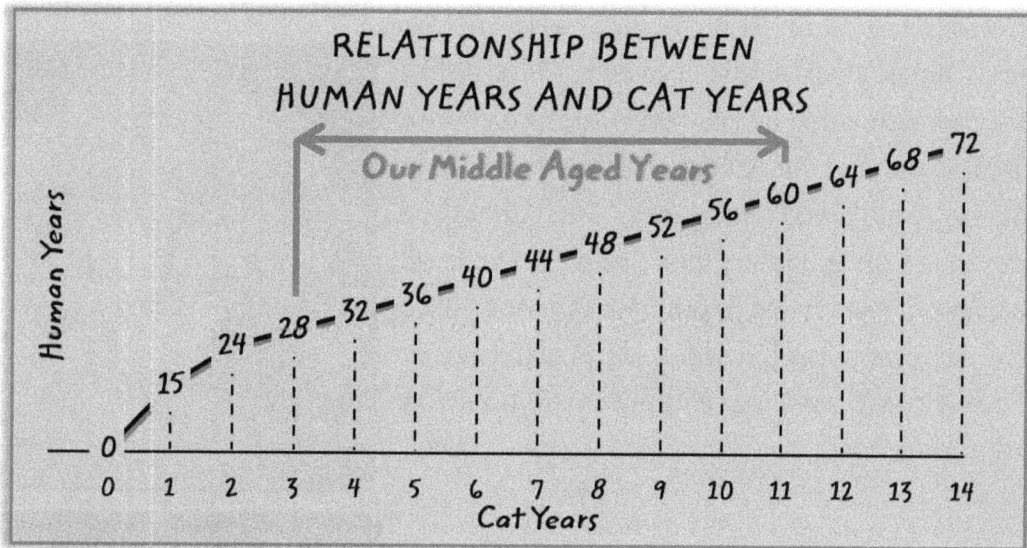

RELATIONSHIP BETWEEN HUMAN YEARS AND CAT YEARS

Our Middle Aged Years

Human Years: 0 — 15 — 24 — 28 — 32 — 36 — 40 — 44 — 48 — 52 — 56 — 60 — 64 — 68 — 72

Cat Years: 0 1 2 3 4 5 6 7 8 9 10 11 12 13 14

This was Kozzie's laid-back phase. He was up for anything, anytime, anywhere, including the manipulation of his ancestor Flyer's large ears, for the enjoyment of others. Whether totally inverted, in bunny mode, or in lamb mode, he was a willing participant and malleable in our hands.

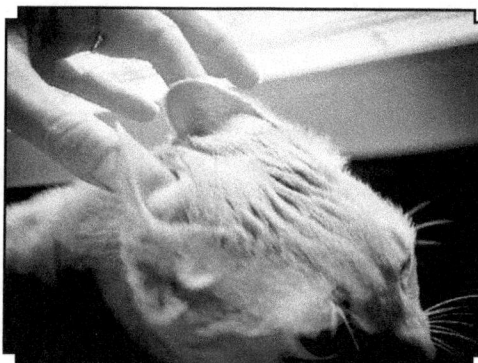

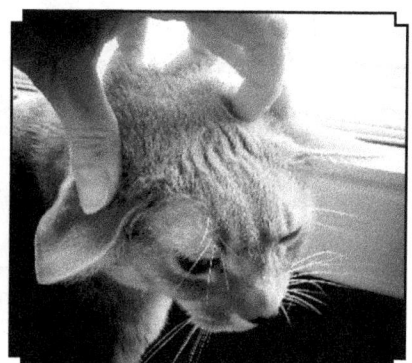

You name it, Koz wore it, and with unfailing stoicism. We took every opportunity to dress him in pint-sized adornments, which often made us laugh until we cried. He was anxious to satisfy his endless curiosity and prove his willingness to be a good sport at the same time.

Kozzie's primary means of long-distance transport was on the shoulders of his six foot, three inch male parent. The lofty position was easy on his paws and gave him a broad view of his kingdom. The few times Koz was allowed outdoors, he surveyed the land while riding his daddy's back as he picked tomatoes from the garden. The two of them had a deep appreciation of living things and were simpatico when it came to nature.

Kozmo checks on crops from the deck

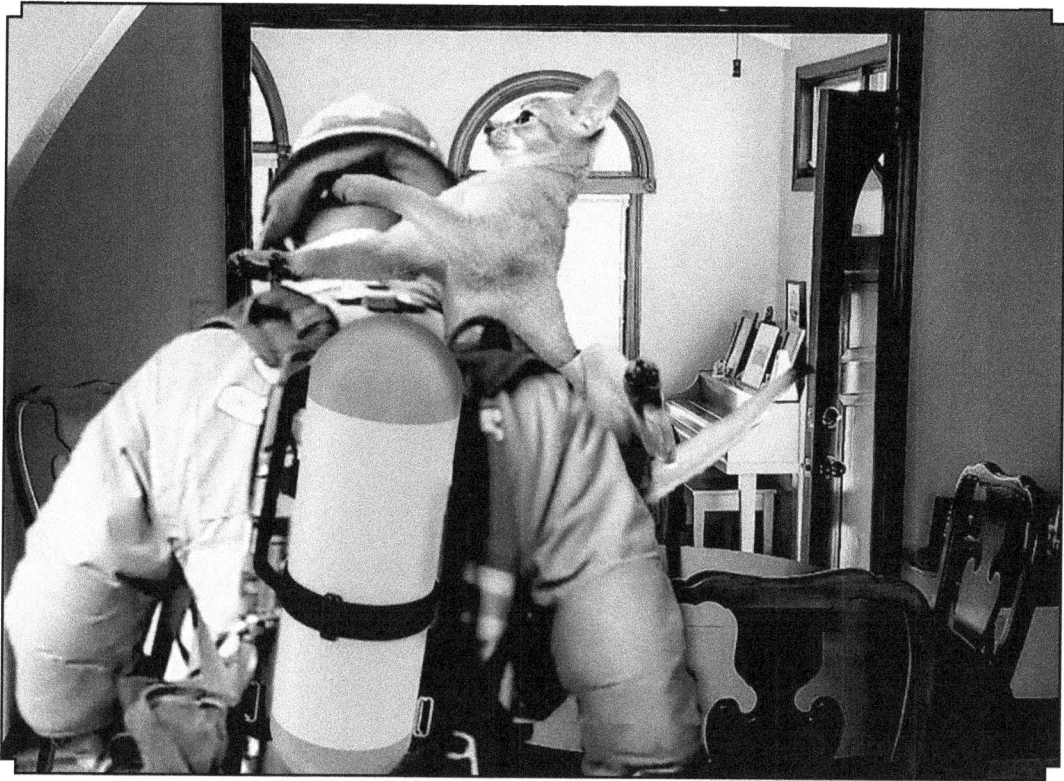

Kozmo loved his sky-high viewpoint so much that he took to jumping on family, friends, and total strangers without their permission or awareness that he would even try such a thing.

Once he did it to a fireman in full uniform. We had arrived home from work one evening to our carbon monoxide detector blaring. We grabbed the cats, fled the house, and called 911.

As the fireman came into the house to check for the gas leak, Koz followed him, jumped on the dining room table, then onto his shoulders. Fortunately, Koz had mounted a cat lover who marveled at his chummy personality. We were relieved when the fireman agreed not to press charges.

As further proof of Kozmo as a cool dude in a loose mood, check out this YouTube web address: **https://youtu.be/MvDeP9K5NaU**

There you will find a video titled *Kozmo's Favorite Things* posted by our daughter, Jill. He loved to be blow-dried, massaged, and vacuumed. Not bragging, just facts.

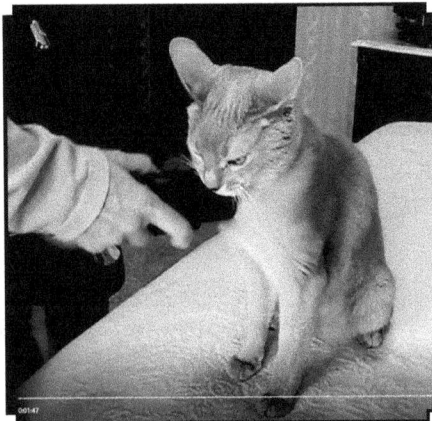

As Kozmo was rewriting the book on clown cat shenanigans, BB was in the shadows, kicking up his own little clouds of dust. The Beeb was not the star, but the straight man in our family feline comedy and was true to his role. Although some of his outward features suggested "in-bread" flaws, there was no question of his subtle strengths. He was on the sidelines, developing his own noteworthy skills apart from the circus act always surrounding his brother.

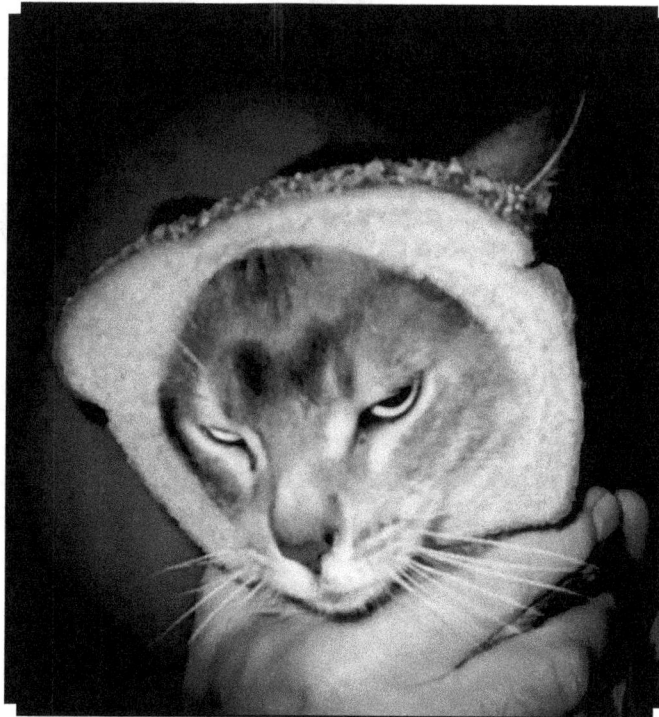

"In-Bread" Beeb

BB was intensely aware of his surroundings at all times, which positioned him at the apex of elite-level household fly catchers. Sometimes he appeared slightly cross-eyed, which no doubt helped his focal prowess in high-speed chases.

Sadly, one of the Beeb's genetic defects was poor teeth, initially unbeknownst to us. He suddenly started shying away from his dry food, hanging his head, and trudging away from the food dish. Our feeding regimen for the boys had always been the free-feed method. It was troubling for us to think that BB may have to be force-fed, especially since he was used to a high-calorie diet (he was always at the bowl). When hugging the little guy one day, we discovered that his right canine tooth was slightly discolored and, on closer inspection, we could actually wiggle it! Off to the vet we went for a dental consultation.

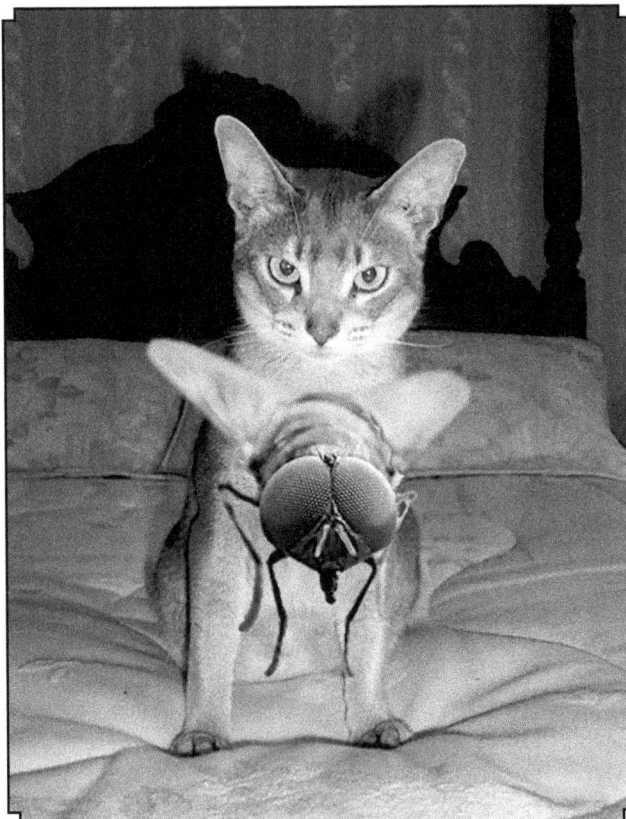

Eyes on the prize

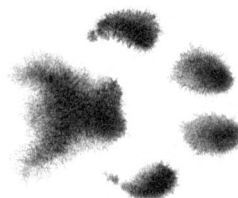

Removal of a cat canine tooth requires anesthetic, so he had to spend the night at the veterinary hospital. While he was under, we had the vet remove a small gray mole that was on top of his head, centered between his ears. Although this was his trademark ID, earning him the handle "Knot Head," we took the opportunity to avoid future issues with it possibly becoming cancerous. The vet told us Abyssinian cats were especially prone to dental problems, so we purchased some chicken-flavored toothpaste and a wee toothbrush and began a preventive dental care program for the boys.

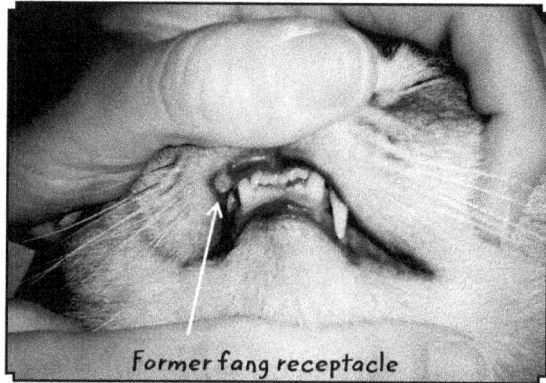

Former fang receptacle

A day at the dentist

Brushing BB's teeth was a difficult two-person job, but Kozmo loved the flavor of the toothpaste so much he was always looking at us for cues indicating it was time to "brush-brush." He was even caught pilfering the tube from the drawer in the bathroom.

7-2-2008 21:33 CST

Surveillance camera Shot 1

7-2-2008 21:34 CST

Surveillance camera Shot 2

It was natural that, as the boys aged, they would develop various maladies, just like their pet parents. One noteworthy instance was when we awoke one morning to Koz sporting a goofy eye. When he was a kitten, Kozmo was treated for eyeball ulcers, so we knew what we were dealing with. After a couple of vet visits without visible signs of healing, his left eye was sewn shut to allow his eyeball to remain saturated in medication and to avoid further contamination.

Another injury

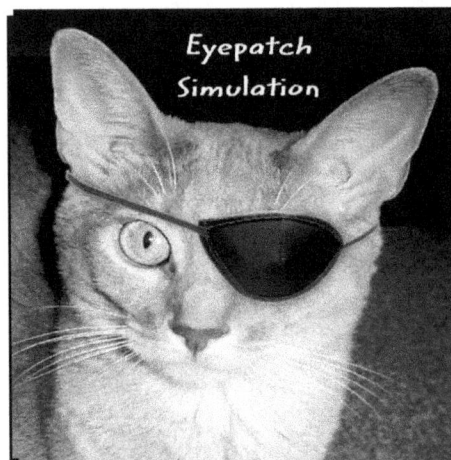

Eyepatch simulation

Since his left lids were sewn together, there was no need for an eyepatch, but it didn't stop us from imagining how he would look and lightening his mood by greeting him with "Arrrgh, Matey!" After a few weeks, his eye was back to normal, but the vet warned us it was possible that, since Kozmo had previous issues with slow healing, he may have an inherited blood disorder called pyruvate kinase deficiency. In layman's terms, it is a form of anemia that causes red blood cells to die prematurely before they can release energy and oxygen to the tissues and organs of affected cats. We could have had him tested for this disease, but there was no treatment or cure. We preferred not to put him through the stress of testing, since it was pointless. We focused on the vigor and enthusiasm he still displayed and relished our time together.

Our family and friends were well aware of our obsession with all things Abyssinian and often gave us Koz-and-BB-related paraphernalia, as if we didn't already have enough. Objects ranged from inch-long gemstone carvings from our longtime friend, Tom, to life-sized dolls handcrafted by my work colleague, Lynn. Kozmo's doll even won first prize at the county fair!

Our treasured keepsakes also included gag gifts, such as a clever yet dark contribution from another work colleague, Kevin. I found evidence of Kevin's feigned anti-feline attitude one day on my desktop. It needed no signature. I knew of only one person with the talent and the odd sense of humor capable of rendering such a creation. It's worthy of sharing.

Kozmo and BB stuffed dolls

Cartoon Kozmo bearing a flattening
treadmark on his back

On the Saturday morning of October 30, 2010, we awoke to a troubling sight. Kozmo had been bleeding internally overnight, and we found him lethargically trudging around the basement near the litter box. Since we'd been warned of the possibility of PKD, we realized the disease was manifesting itself as we saw his bloody stool. The timing of this event was bad. We were up early that day to make a two-hour drive to celebrate Jim's mother Arlene's ninety-third birthday, and we were a key part of the family tasked with pulling it off.

There was no choice. We had to travel as planned. Humans before pets: a motto we didn't want to uphold at the time, but did. We prepared a comfy spot for Koz near his food, water, and litter box. We were relieved to see him eat and drink a bit just before we hit the road.

Needless to say, our thoughts during that day were not focused on Arlene, but we did our due diligence as cheerful participants in her birthday party. We didn't let her know about our dilemma at the time. She was one of Kozmo's biggest fans, and, if told of his condition, she would have demanded we stay with him and take him to the vet instead of attending her special event.

Kozmo and Grandma Arlene
celebrate Christmas 2009

Upon our arrival back home, we found Koz, still in the basement, with his head raised from a tightly-tucked position to welcome us. It was after nine o'clock at night, but we bundled him up in a blanket and took him to a twenty-four hour emergency pet care facility not far away. He appeared weak but responsive to our coos of concern along the way, which gave us hope that our delay had not caused him negative consequences.

After getting a quick summary of Kozmo's health history concerning the possibility of PKD, the staff took him from us to test his blood. We sat in the waiting room with another family whose dog was in surgery after having been struck by a car. The human anguish in the room was palpable.

The vet returned to verify that Kozzie's blood indicated PKD. His internal bleeding had left him even more anemic than his chronic condition had already caused. To improve, he would need a blood transfusion to raise his red blood cell count. Although the care facility kept a few pet cats of its own to use as emergency blood donors, none of them had a compatible blood type. They could sedate him, give him fluids, and keep him until our own vet opened on Monday morning.

With heavy hearts, we drove home alone to an unsettled BB brother. We shared his worry about his best buddy but began our plan of what to do come Monday.

We were at the door of our own vet clinic when it opened, after gathering Kozmo up from the emergency clinic. He was groggy, but we could tell he was very glad to see us. Kozmo's favorite vet was near retirement, and we were happy it was her in the office that day when we entered. She, like all of his intimates, was smitten with him and immediately remembered his impish character. She was shocked to see him in such condition. We passed on his file of medical details and asked if his brother, BB, could be a blood donor for him, since he and Koz had a common ancestor in Flyer. We had brought the Beeb with us just in case this was an option.

After BB's blood test, we were disheartened to find there was not an acceptable match between their types. The vet did another test of Kozzie's red blood count and discovered it hadn't declined since the test taken at the emergency clinic. She considered this relatively good news, though she had to remove some of his precious life fluid to test it. She added more fluid under his skin by syringe, which left a temporary, Quasimodo-like bump that would gradually be assimilated into his system. She said it was possible to send his blood sample to an organization in California that matched unusual types, but it would take several days to send the sample, type it, try to find a possible donor match, and, if there was one, send it back to us. Since Kozmo's blood count had not changed in thirty-six hours, she said we could take him home and return the next day, hoping for improvement.

So that's what we did. We took him back to the basement so he could stay close to the litter box. He was a fastidious little guy and had never made a toiletry error since the first day of his adoption. He proved to us that he wasn't going to start making messes now. Once settled in the comfortable nest we created for him, he slowly stood up and wobbled his way to his box, climbing in to do his duty. It brought us to tears, seeing him struggle so. A mere two days ago he had been his vibrant, bright-eyed, mischievous self, and now he was obviously dizzy and weak, but still able to boom out that clattering purr we loved so much, which calmed us somewhat.

This is the last photo taken of Kozmo, lying quietly on his blanket. His right paw had been shaved days before for his tests and intravenous lines. It looked as though he was wearing a wee UGG boot in a fashionable sand color, exhibiting his quintessential dapper presence to the nth degree.

Last photo of Kozmo

Since I was still working and Jim was retired, he was Kozmo's day nurse. We had gotten a feeding syringe from the vet to make sure Koz was getting nourishment during this rough time. The first day he was home, he accepted some small doses of wet food, but wasn't really interested in eating. We supplied water to him by syringe as well, since he was still so shaky on his feet.

We took him back to the vet the following day. His blood count remained the same, no worse but no better, and he seemed to be in stable condition. We took him home again, but our hopes were low.

From then on, our time was spent in the basement with him, and we accepted it as our new family room. The Beeb was close by his side, but didn't try to nuzzle. Even the Beeb recognized his fragile condition. We continued taking Koz to the vet for the next two days. His blood count was steady, but his increasing weakness was visible as he tried to stand without success. He accepted less and less food, and on Thursday evening he was unable to use the litter box, wetting his blanket. He looked at us in humiliation. Our family foursome agreed his condition the following morning would dictate his fate.

On Friday, November 5, a week after Kozmo had started his downward spiral, we arrived again at the vet's office. He was so weak; we didn't ask for another test. Even if it had been another stable result, it was obvious we needed to let go of his tiny, wavering spirit.

This experience was every bit as painful as the loss of my mother. It was also unbelievably coincidental that both of these loved ones would share the same ultimate cause of death: extreme anemia. Jim was so devastated, he may as well have had a mortal wound, bleeding out in front of me. Our compassionate vet was crying along with us as we nodded for her to release Kozmo to his next voyage. A technician brought a tiny quilt, just taken from a warm clothes dryer, and laid it on the examination table. The vet gently placed Koz on the quilt and laid another over his legs and torso. We sobbed as we talked to him, praising his unique qualities and promising to always remember him. As was his style, he saved us even more agonizing pain by closing his eyes before his last breath.

We asked the vet to cremate Kozmo's earthly shell. Upon getting his cremains in a package a few days later, Jim reached into the box to grab the bag holding what was left of him. It held the handful of minerals which was once our warm, wee fuzzling. Jim seldom looked for a tangible spiritual connection to our pets, but he swore to me that, when he picked up the bag, he felt a tingle run through his hand. For me to experience such a reaction was to be expected, but he would never have admitted such a thing if it hadn't actually happened. The bag Kozzie was in had a quote from a poem "The Rainbow Bridge" embroidered on it. There are many versions of this poem, and they all consist of comforting words to those who mourn human and animal losses.

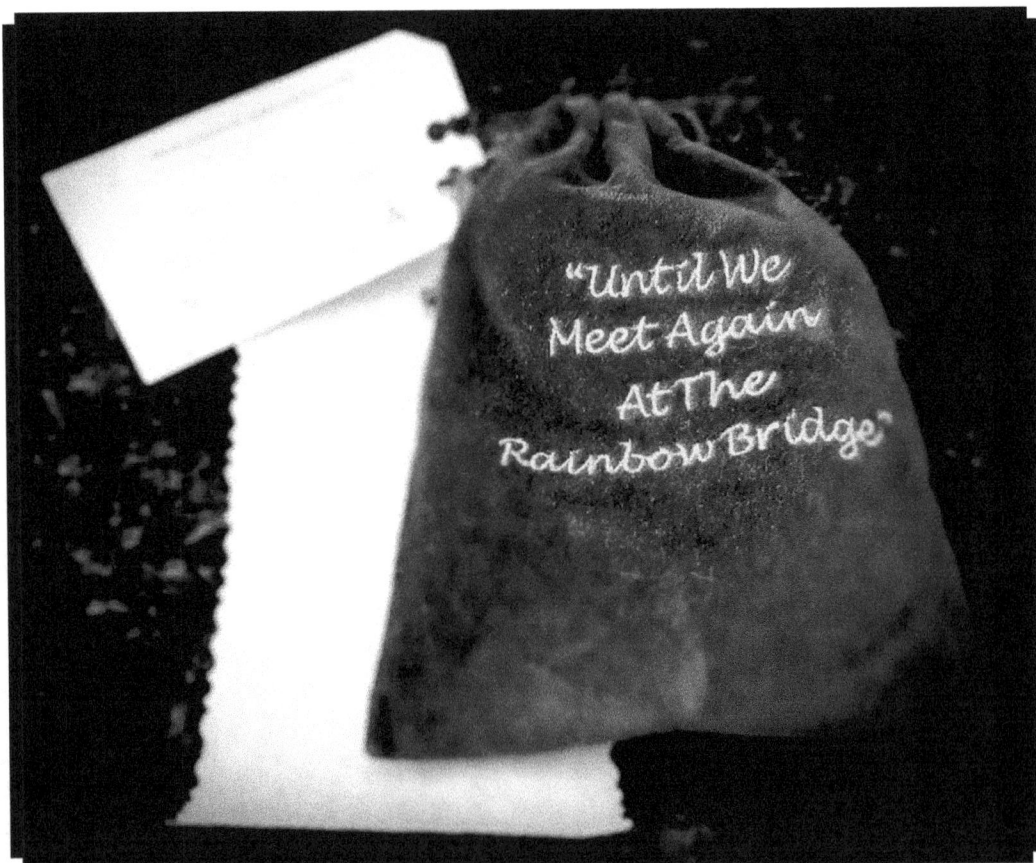

A different poem I've found is one that greatly comforts me and keeps my memories of my favorite people and pets vivid. When I, myself, go to the great beyond, I hope those who care about me think of me in these terms.

Death Is Nothing at All...

Death is nothing at all.
It does not count.
I have only slipped away into the next room.
Nothing has happened.

Everything remains exactly as it was.
I am I, and you are you,
and the old life that we lived so fondly together is untouched, unchanged.
Whatever we were to each other, that we are still.

Call me by the old familiar name.
Speak of me in the easy way which you always used.
Put no difference into your tone.
Wear no forced air of solemnity or sorrow.

Laugh as we always laughed
at the little jokes that we enjoyed together.
Play, smile, think of me, pray for me.
Let my name be ever the household word that it always was.

Let it be spoken without an effort,
without the ghost of a shadow upon it.
Life means all that it ever meant.
It is the same as it ever was.

There is absolute and unbroken continuity.

What is this death but a negligible accident?

Why should I be out of mind

because I am out of sight?

I am but waiting for you,

for an interval,

somewhere very near,

just round the corner.

All is well.

Nothing is hurt; nothing is lost.

One brief moment and all will be as it was before.

How we shall laugh at the trouble of parting when we meet again![/poem]

Henry Scott Holland, 1847-1918

[Editor's Note: Excerpt from his sermon titled *Death the King of Terrors* in May 1910 following the death of King Edward VII.]

Chapter 10: Nov. 2010-Oct. 2013, Circle of Life

There was no doubt in our minds that particles of Kozmo's spirit were washing over us every day. That is the lightest, kindest aspect of memory, although welcoming fond recollections brings with them the weight of darker times as well. It takes practice to focus on the wonderful while acknowledging but releasing the painful. The passing of beloved pets can be opportunities to value the circle of life of all creatures and treasure those we care for most passionately.

Clay memorial Kozmo
sculpture by Kris

Jim, the Beeb, and I were emotionally empty due to Kozmo's loss. BB searched for him everywhere, confused by how much his little world had changed but not understanding why. We shared that confusion, battling our brains to quit seeing Kozzie from the corners of our eyes as we schlepped through the motions of our daily lives.

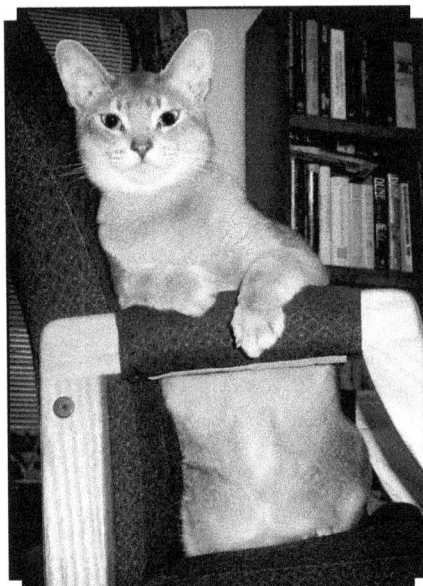

As the days passed, we realized more and more that BB always had the makings of a perfect pet cat. I had often credited him as a deep thinker (to the chuckles of family and friends), but he quickly proved me right, especially to his doubting daddy.

One morning, while applying my face to greet the day, Beeb followed me into the bathroom and jumped up on the counter to request his morning drink from the faucet, Kozmo-style.

BB getting a drink Kozmo-Style

He noticed me primping in front of the magnifying side of my makeup mirror and froze. Then he cautiously approached the mirror, apparently not sure if what he saw was friend or foe.

Once he recognized himself in the mirror, he slowly crept closer. Then he started checking himself out.

First, he turned his head and took a good, long look at his left side...

...then he switched to take a peek at his right side...

...then full-frontal.

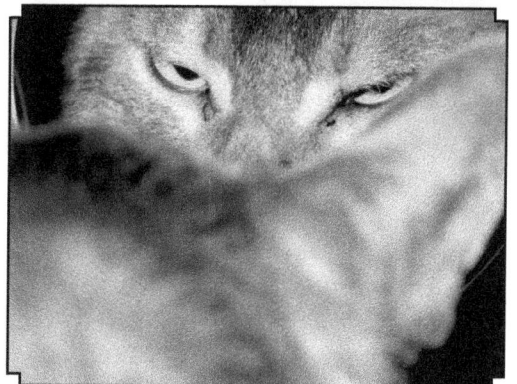

He met his own eyes, reflected in the mirror, then gradually did a visual sweep of his forehead, cheeks, and chin. Then he turned and looked at me, real face to real face. He and I had made eye contact in mirrors many times, but I think this was the first time he put it together with reality. Yep, a deep thinker.

Hmmm...now **THIS** looks like some quality television.

With his big brother gone, BB took to shadowing Jim and me as Kozmo substitutes for how and where to spend his waking hours. If I was on the home computer, he was on my lap, either pawing at the cursor as I moused or watching letters appear out of nowhere as I typed. One of his wildest psychological rides was when I was viewing a digital movie of him chasing his latest favorite toy mouse. As the Beeb watched himself on the computer monitor, I took pictures of him digesting the subject matter as it sunk in.

Hey, wait a minute...

Hey, wait a minute...

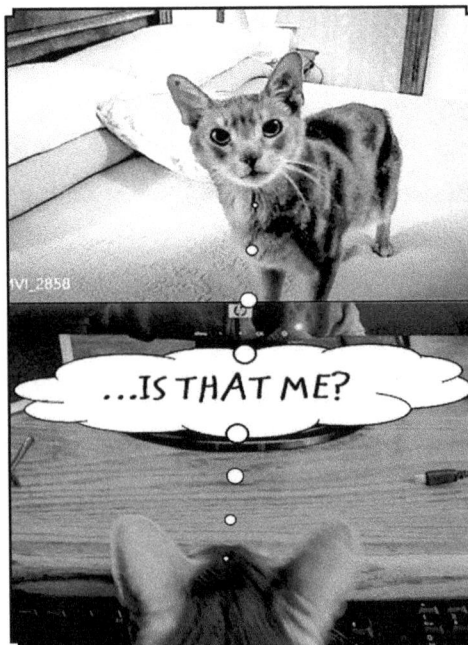

...IS THAT ME?

For a look at the video of the Beeb watching himself, go to the following YouTube address to watch "Memoir of BB:"

https://youtu.be/C7-4WO-Afrw

Even wee, sweet Beeb wasn't immune to health issues. A couple of years after Kozmo's passing, he developed symptoms of weight loss, fatigue and listlessness. The vet diagnosed him with pancreatitis. When inflamed, his pancreas interrupted the flow of enzymes into his digestive tract and forced them out into other areas of his digestive system which, in effect, caused his body to digest itself. Thankfully, BB responded well to treatment, which extended his life for about a year after his diagnosis. We were warned to watch for sudden visible discomfort he may have, since signs of his medication becoming ineffective could progress rapidly.

It was clear the Beeb was able to enjoy his life again once treated, but knowing his days were numbered prompted us to value his loving companionship and endearing traits more than ever before.

About a month after filming "Memoir of BB," his mood suddenly changed and he stopped eating. His discomfort was very clear to us, and we knew the decision we were dreading was at hand. BB's vet was tenderly involved in his treatment and offered to come to our home when it was time to ease his pain. Unfortunately, she was out of town when we needed her.

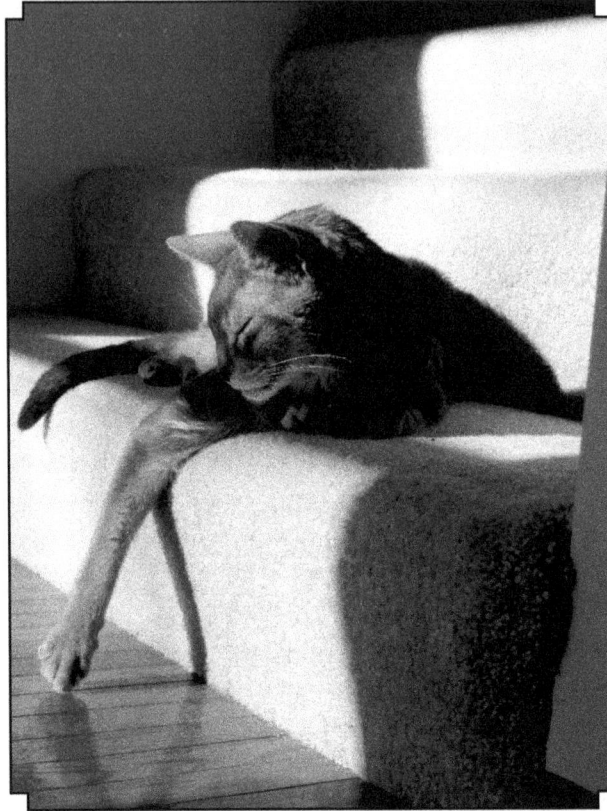

We followed the practiced path we had taken on Kozmo's last day and bundled up our listless friend, taking him to the vet for the last time. We were glad we had recognized BB's failing faculties soon after they appeared so his pain could be overcome with a welcome release, which we met with stifled sobs as he faded from us.

Now our home was hauntingly quiet as we sat, absorbing the finality of our obligatory decision. I closed my eyes and remembered the feeling of the Beeb's warm breath on my forehead as I practiced my daily corpse yoga pose with my eyes closed. He had a habit of hovering his face over mine as I lay prone and motionless on the floor. I suppose he was checking me for signs of life. I would always open my eyes when I felt his presence, calming his fears. He would make eye contact, turn, then amble away, satisfied I was still alive.

I made a card to send to our family and friends announcing BB's loss with this message:

When the box with the embroidered pouch holding the Beeb's ashes arrived in the mail, we placed it gently atop Kozmo's cremains in a wooden crypt we still display in memoriam of our special Abyssinian boys.

There was a vacuum in our hearts where the Beeb used to be, and it was hard to ignore. It had been twenty-five years since we had been catless, and we were initially clueless about how best to deal with it. We didn't want to continue without the uplifting feeling of sharing our woes and celebrations alike with our fuzz-wuzzies, who always met us at the door, ready to whisk us away with them to live in the moment.

Within a few weeks, we were scouring our resources, looking for two Abyssinian kittens within a day's drive. We were surprised to discover we couldn't find any. We tried searching for a breeder off and on for six months with no luck. Our need for furry companionship was so great that we decided the breed wasn't really important. On the spur of the moment one October day, we hopped into the car and drove the two miles to our local pet adoption center. We had no idea if it was a good time of year to look for kittens, but that was what we were interested in getting. We felt we should start with a young cat to ease back into pet parenting and hoped we would end up finding one with a personality similar to that of our precocious Abyssinians.

There were about fifteen kittens available for us to pick from. We strolled along the tasteful windowed compartments, tapping on the glass and gauging the reactions of the occupants. We passed one with a wee occupant named Marty, a male, who was asleep with his back to the customers. He was the same luscious caramel color of Kozmo, which immediately caught our attention. We tapped and tapped on the glass, but got no reaction. We moved on, thinking the little guy was way too tame for us clown-cat lovers. After checking all contenders, we asked to see three different kittens in an available viewing room along with an accompanying shelter aide that could access their history by computer. We eventually narrowed our choice to a gray tabby. Then Jim said, "I think we should take a look at that little tan one."

This took some effort. Marty was under quarantine. He had been a three-month-old stray when he was brought to the shelter with every undesirable defect possible: fleas, worms, an eye infection, a cold, and even a couple of bites out of one ear. He had been living at the shelter for a month, recovering from all of his maladies, and was finally ready to adopt, but couldn't yet be mixed with other kittens.

Jim thought he was still worth a look, so the attendant woke him up and brought him to us in the quarantine room. He had a beautiful coat of fluffy fur, mostly fawn-colored but swirled with a darker tan on his legs and haunches. He also had a two-toned nose pad, liver-colored above and light pink around his nostrils. His eyes were deep amber and slightly closed, giving him a somewhat put-upon look. When the aide set him on the floor, he still looked a little sleepy, but Jim threw a toy mouse at him and he exploded in a blur of motion in front of our eyes. He was riotously funny. We all laughed out loud at his antics. Jim picked him up and Marty cuddled in, looking Jim in the eyes. Then he promptly fell asleep again.

We adopted our first member of
Generation Z minutes later.

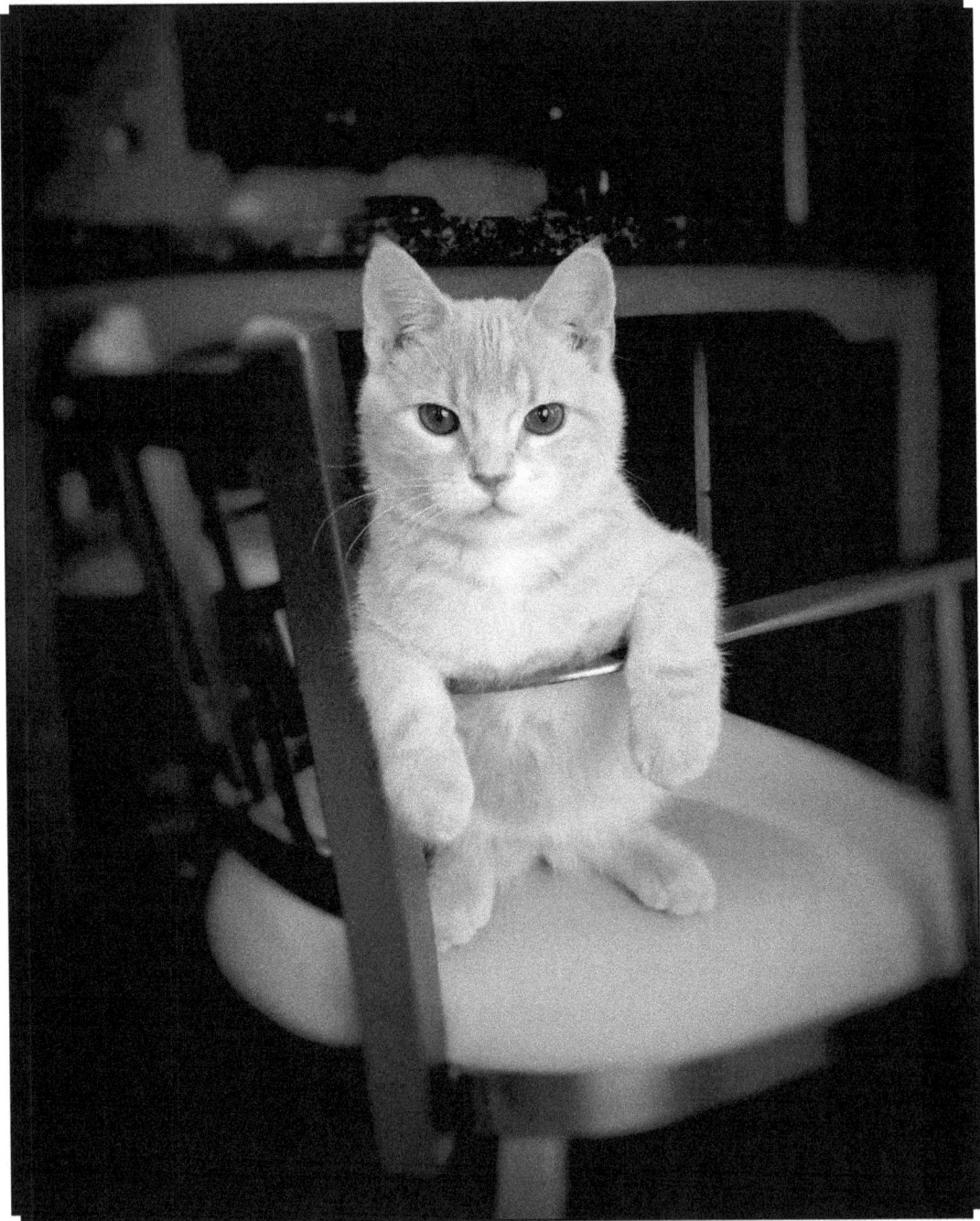

While waiting to get our new kitty cat, I mused upon the potential names I had been archiving to bestow upon our next furball. First on the list was "Peachuz," which also happened to be Jim's favorite fruit pie. This was rejected, since I thought it was best suited for a female cat. Though Marty was neutered, he was way too boisterous for a name like Peachuz. Next on the list was "Smacky," which was the name of Bucky the Siamese cat's favorite teddy bear in the newspaper comic "Get Fuzzy." I decided that Smacky was more of a unisex name, but considered it still in the running.

The last selection in my naming list was "Munk," after Monkey Chadwick. He played the belligerent chimp hand puppet, voiced and manipulated by ventriloquist Nina Conti, in HBO's comedy series *Family Tree*. He (they) was (were) my favorite(s) character(s) on the show. For some odd reason, "Munk" struck a chord with me, though at the time of naming I didn't understand why. Jim thought it a bizarre choice, but had known for some time that it was on my cat-name shortlist and gave in to me, even before deliberating.

Our newly-named "Munk" with his own
"Smacky" surrogate

Munk's namesake, Monkey Chadwick and
his "Handler" ventriloquist Nina Conti

By the time we got home, Munk had nearly ripped himself out of the cardboard box he had been put in at the shelter. We set the box on the floor of the living room and opened it the rest of the way. He shot out of it as if from a cartoon cat cannon. I missed his initial antics as I broke for the bathroom, my bladder about to burst after the two-hour pet selection process. I was nearly relieved of the internal pressure, when, much to my surprise, the wee rascal plip-plopped on tiny paws through the slightly open bathroom door, squatted in front of me, looked me straight in the eye, and made a small organic creation on the ceramic-tiled floor. It was his destiny after all, as foretold by the first adoptive moments of both Kozmo and the Beeb. Ah, we were back in the saddle again!

Watch for the sequel, "Munk, Master of Cute" coming soon!

www.ingramcontent.com/pod-product-compliance
Lightning Source LLC
Chambersburg PA
CBHW081551040426
42448CB00016B/3289